THE
HOME POTTER

by

IAN LAUDER

UNIVERSE BOOKS
New York

Published in the United States of
America in 1971 by Universe Books
381 Park Avenue South, New York,
N.Y. 10016
© Ian Lauder 1970

Library of Congress Catalog Card
Number: 71 130802

ISBN 0 87663 136 7

Printed in Great Britain

DEDICATION

To my parents, without whom there would have been no pots,
and to my wife,
who put up with the mess.

CONTENTS

FOREWORD

I have learned practically everything I know about pottery the hard way, by trial and error. I have never attended classes. I have, however, read a few books on the subject. At times it has all been maddeningly frustrating. Now after about five years I believe that at last I have overcome nearly all my difficulties. There has been much work, much disappointment but, I am glad to say, also much satisfaction in reaching this stage. On looking back through the books which I have acquired to aid me in my apprenticeship, I do not think there is one which gave all the answers to the day to day problems which confronted me. All were full of most valuable information, much of it for advanced students, but no single book seemed to deal in a language which I could understand, with all the troubles I encountered during my faltering progress. Perhaps I was more than usually unfortunate in my experiences. Still, I feel sure there must be others who could be saved some of the disasters, some of the pitfalls, which for me were, alas, all too frequent.

In the process of becoming a potter I have collected a number of simple ideas, ways of dealing with everyday crises, call them 'wrinkles' if you will, which I have not seen mentioned elsewhere. Perhaps others thought they were so well-known, so elementary, that they were not worth recording. I have recorded them. I hope that they will prove useful to beginners.

I realise that there are many people who would like to take an interest in pottery but who find headway slow and restricted at evening classes due to the limitations imposed through shortage of equipment. No one can hope to learn how to throw properly, having access to a power wheel for only a few minutes once a week. The kiln is hardly ever available for experiment in such classes and is seldom controlled by the students themselves. I have, therefore, devoted some space to describing a potter's wheel which is not too difficult to build and a very simple little kiln which can be assembled in a few hours for a fraction of the cost of the commercial product. I have used both myself.

It is my hope that with the aid of this equipment much truly interesting and creative work can be done. I think we owe no less to this, perhaps, the oldest craft of all.

Disley 1969

1
CLAY

The basic substance of all pottery is clay. Fortunately for us it is found in almost every country in the world. It is usually near the surface so is relatively easy to obtain and quite cheap. It can be divided into two distinct categories: primary clay which is mined precisely where the material was originally formed from decayed volcanic rock millions of years ago; and secondary clays which have been carried in suspension in rivers or by other means, later to be deposited far from their old sites. Secondary clays are the more common and, in fact, there are very few counties in Britain where clay of this type is not readily available. If there is none in your own garden you should not have far to travel to find it in abundance. It is easy to collect clay from fruitful sources of supply, building excavations or local road works; sometimes the material exposed is suitable for pottery, sometimes it is not. A great deal depends upon the impurities which it has collected during its long journey from the place where it was originally evolved. No less than three-fifths of the earth's crust is composed of clay. It is reasonable to assume that quite a large proportion of this total is usable in one form or another, which makes it difficult to imagine a manufacturing substance, a raw material, which is so conveniently available, so easy to acquire.

Clay is to be found almost everywhere and we shall presently see how it can be collected, treated and refined. Although there are many commercial stockists from whom supplies can be obtained by those who do not wish to go to the trouble of winning their own, there is no doubt that much greater satisfaction is to be gained by employing a product which you have completely prepared yourself.

Pure clay is by no means the only ingredient used in the making of pottery. Others are needed to decorate it by the application of various pigments, and to glaze it with a coating which will make it impervious to water. They offer the opportunity to improve the product, making the finished article more attractive and more useful, and afford the potter a chance to express his own individualism in an altogether uninhibited way.

Besides being cheap, clay has many other important properties. The most attractive of these is its plasticity. That is to say it is easily malleable into any shape. Once formed it will retain that shape until further pressure is applied. With a good clay this plastic property can be controlled by the addition of water and it is simple in this way to adjust its behaviour to suit circumstances. For example, fashioned into a primitive container or bowl, clay can be allowed to dry whereupon it becomes rigid. Such crude vessels used to be kept in this condition for the storage of grain and many other substances. If the pot were broken in service, it was only necessary to wet the pieces and then start all over again. Not only can clay be reclaimed many times, but it actually improves on each occasion; it never wears out; it becomes still more plastic. When you start potting seriously you will always keep a bucket for scrap lumps and broken pots which will all be re-used later.

Only when clay has been heated in a kiln does it change completely to become hard and brittle. This process alters the chemical structure of the material. It is irreversible and the basis of all pottery. Never again can the fired pot be softened by water because an entirely new substance has been formed. This new material is utterly stable and is one which will endure for thousands of years. Even today archaeologists are excavating pottery which was made in ancient cities long before the Pyramids were built on the banks of the Nile. Ur of the Chaldees has yielded shards whose red clay body is just as strong and durable now as when it first emerged from some primitive kiln at the very beginning of civilisation. The humble plant pot will last just as long.

Who first thought of firing clay we shall never know. We cannot even fix with certainty the race who discovered the process. Possibly, like so many other human inventions, it was a pure accident. We can imagine that a container of one form or another was left by chance in a fire. Perhaps it was somehow forgotten until the following morning when the ashes were being raked aside. The new found properties it had acquired would have been quickly appreciated. More pieces would have been placed in fires to see if the same effect could be repeated. So, perhaps, pottery began.

I do not think it would be right for this little book to describe at length the chemical composition of clay and its auxiliaries. Nevertheless, one should have a little basic information about the materials which one is using if the fullest benefit from the practice is to be obtained. I hope, therefore, that the reader will not skip the next few paragraphs.

Clay in its simplest form is nothing more than powdered rock. It is, however, a special type of rock which has been heated by volcanic action, granite for example. Gradually masses of such rock were forced to the surface due to upheavals deep down in the earth's crust until they became exposed to the weather. It was then that the incredibly slow process of disintegration began. The ultimate product after millions of years is a very finely divided material—clay—consisting mainly of silica and alumina. Silica is a compound of silicon and oxygen (sand) and alumina is the metal aluminium combined with oxygen. The primary white deposits of Cornwall, Devon and Dorset have remained *in situ* since their formation and have not been contaminated by impurities. The secondary clays which, as we have seen, are far more widespread, have collected a host of chemicals such as salts of iron which make them red, or they may be coloured grey or black due to the presence of carbonaceous materials which are the product of the decay of the profuse plant life in the swamps which covered our land so many centuries ago.

Scientists are not altogether agreed as to the exact reason for clay having this convenient property of plasticity. One theory, which seems to be reasonably tenable, is that the particles behave as though they exist in the form of flat flakes. It is said that, so long as there are globules of water between them, the flakes slide smoothly over each other. The amount of internal friction varies with the quantity of moisture present. As the clay dries, the flakes make contact and the friction increases. The removal of further water results in the globules disappearing altogether, the pot becomes rigid since the lubricating medium has been lost and it contracts. If water is added again, dampening the clay, it flows back between the flakes, plasticity is restored and the piece begins to resume its original size.

When clay is heated in a kiln a series of chemical changes take place culminating in the formation of the new material which, in the trade, is known as *biscuit ware*. First, however, there is a progressive loss of free moisture, up to a temperature of about 120 degs. centigrade. The water inside the body is being boiled away. Outwardly the pot then appears perfectly dry. In fact it still contains more moisture which is chemically combined in such a way that it cannot be totally released until a temperature of 700 degs. centigrade has been reached. In the meantime small organic particles, which are mixed with all clays to some extent, burn away leaving the material very porous indeed. It has now passed the point of no return. It can never be dissolved in water again. It is still not good pot because it is far too soft and the texture coarse and open. It must therefore be heated still further. During this final stage to at least 1000 degs. centigrade, the pot contracts again because the pores diminish in size whilst the alumina combines with the silica to form a stable compound— aluminium silicate. The clay has now been biscuit fired. It has been changed into pottery. In a later chapter we shall see how these processes can be controlled.

If we were to visit a modern commercial pottery, we would, very likely, see only white clay. This is *body* which has been blended from a number of different ingredients. It is certainly not the simple product direct from the mines of the South West. Some of the additives are flint, quartz and sand, which along with other chemicals, control the behaviour of the clay when it is being worked or fired. Thus the supplier is in a position to offer the potter materials which will best suit his particular processes or firing procedure. The preparation of clay, therefore, has now become a highly specialised industry supported by all the resources of the modern chemical laboratory. Yet, in spite of these rather formidable advances of modern science, it is still possible to prove that ordinary garden clay can be used otherwise than for growing roses. If you are fortunate enough to have access to a few shovelfuls of the right stuff, we shall now see how it can be put to good use.

2
DIGGING YOUR BODY

Clay is well-known to the gardener. It is easily distinguishable from soil because it tends to be brown or yellow rather than black. It sticks to the spade or forms large plastic lumps which slice smoothly. It is heavy and dense; sometimes it is a great nuisance. Take a piece and squeeze it in the hand: it should leave a faithful impression. Wet the surface and pass the fingers across it: it should feel quite slippy. Work a small piece until it is soft and pliable, bend it a little: it should not crack. An ordinary lump of clay dug straight from the rose bed with the above properties may, as an experiment, be fired in a kiln just as it is. It must be heated slowly to a good red heat and then allowed to cool equally slowly. It will be found to have become a piece of pot. True, the result will be rough and crude, it may have cracked and warped, it will be uneven and ugly but it is still pot.

Obviously, in order to be able to make useful articles, clay must undergo a minimum of treatment aimed at removing all foreign matter which is not strictly clay. Some impurities will have to remain, but many of these as a·rule do little harm and are quite acceptable to the potter.

Secondary clay deposits are frequently found on or close to the surface; they may be many feet thick. There is often much contamination with carbonaceous substances derived from plant debris and soil; lower down there will probably be sand and pebbles. Sand in limited amounts will do no harm as it consists of almost pure silica and, when evenly distributed throughout the body, it gives strength and firmness to the clay being worked. Commercially prepared bodies are often conditioned to achieve similar effects by the insertion of *grog* (crushed fired clay).

To save unnecessary work, one naturally selects a bed where the clay is concentrated and as free as possible from obvious inclusions. Having collected the required quantity, this should be broken down with a trowel or the hands into lumps of about one inch cube. In doing this, one tends to expose entrained stones which will then be easy to remove. Any other intruders can be dealt with at the same time.

It is usually recommended that clay should be allowed to lie weathering for up to two years after being dug before it is refined. This is said to break up the surface through the action of sun, rain and frost, so improving its properties. Therefore, if supplies can be collected from an old building site or road excavation so much the better, but the author must admit to digging, treating and firing samples of local clay all in less than three weeks. The results were surprisingly good, but perhaps he was just lucky.

Tip the lumps into a large basin or bucket and cover with water. In a few hours the material will soften which can be encouraged by stirring, until the whole mass has the consistency of a soft brown mud or *slurry*, as it is called. More stones will probably now make their presence felt and it is convenient to get rid of them before sieving.

The sieve should have a lawn with a number 80 mesh or the nearest available. A domestic cooking sieve is usually much too coarse. The best way to hold the device over the bucket is by supporting it on a couple of sticks or laths (figure 1). As a substitute, the home potter can use a cloth such as the one

FIG. 1   FIG. 2

found in the kitchen for drying glasses. Suspend it from the four legs of an upturned chair (figure 2) and position a washing up bowl or other suitable receptacle underneath.

Since the slurry will contain much abrasive material, great care is needed to avoid tearing the cloth. To promote flow through the filter, the mass must be gently brushed backwards and forwards as each few cupfuls are deposited into the cloth. From

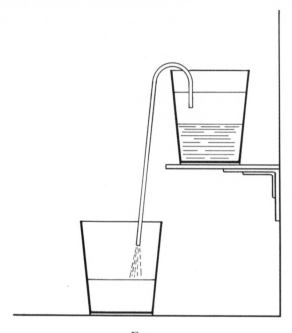

FIG. 3

time to time remove the residue which is clearly not going to pass through and later throw it away. The container underneath should collect a dark brown watery solution; there is no harm in using a little extra water to wash the clay through the cloth if it seems too thick and sluggish.

The liquid must now be left to stand for some hours, the longer the better as this will give the finer particles time to settle to the bottom and it is to these that most clays owe their plasticity. The sand of course will drop in the first hour but this is little use without the binding effect of the other suspended material. At

17

the end of a week, for example, if the bucket has not been dis-
turbed, the water will be quite clear near the top and become
progressively more cloudy the deeper one goes. The excess
water should now be siphoned off with a rubber tube, leaving
about one quarter of the original volume at the bottom (figure 3).

There are a number of ways of eliminating the remaining
water. One is by evaporation, allowing it to be driven off by
warming (not boiling) on a fire or stove. This can go a long way
to freeing the clay of moisture and the final stage is to press out
the last cupful or so between cloths. Heating, however, is
inclined to be expensive if a large quantity is involved and it is
much simpler and better to use a slab of plaster. Ordinary
domestic plaster of Paris is a very porous substance capable of
claiming surprisingly large amounts of water if a wet mass is
placed in contact with it.

To make a plaster slab, mix about 20 lb. of decorator's finishing
plaster with water in a bucket and keep stirring until it shows
signs of being ready to set. Always sprinkle plaster into water,
never vice versa. Now pour about two-thirds of the plaster into
the lid of a rigid box which has sides at least four inches high.
Make sure before doing so that it is watertight, and plug the
leaks with soft clay, where necessary. When the bottom is
covered to a depth of 2 inches allow the plaster to harden a little
before trowelling out the rest from the bucket and building up
the sides to form a rather thick tray or sink (figure 4). Scrap
plaster should never be discharged down drains as it tends to
cause blockages unless great care is taken. Leave it in the dustbin
or bury it.

The 'sink' will set quite quickly and soon will be hard. It

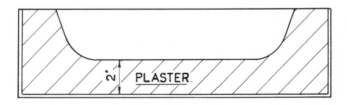

FIG. 4

should now be kept in a warm dry atmosphere for a day or two to drive away all the moisture. When ready for use stir the mixture of clay and water vigorously to distribute the various sizes of particles and then quickly pour into the sink and leave to stand. In a little while, it will be noticed that the level is beginning to fall and a thin film of brown clay is starting to collect along the sides. After some hours there will be a slab of clay which will start to contract away from the edges of the plaster sink as it dries and can be easily removed. The first part of the preparation is complete.

Although at this stage the clay may look serviceable, in fact it still needs some attention before it will be much use for making pottery. It has to be *wedged*. For this one needs a firm table or bench, preferably one with sides which will prevent the spattering of other objects in the room. If possible a thin strong brass wire may be stretched across to be used for cutting the clay (a strong nylon fishing line is a very good substitute for a wire). The wire may be separate if this is more convenient. Now take a lump of clay weighing, say, 4 lb. (less if only a small quantity has been prepared), form it into a ball with the hands and cut it through the centre with the wire. Place one half on the table with the cut face pointing away, raise the other half above your head and bring it down (figure 5) with as much force as possible on to the clay on the table. When they strike, the two cut sides should be roughly in line. Gather up the whole mass, work it back into the shape of a ball and repeat the exercise. The above ritual should go on until, when the wire slices through the clay, the cut face is perfectly smooth and free from any holes. Usually at least thirty cuts are needed and the harder the two pieces are slammed together the quicker will the air bubbles be dispersed. If any bubbles are allowed to remain, they are apt to make throwing on the wheel more difficult, and any which are trapped below the surface when the piece is put in the kiln will expand with heat, exerting enormous pressure possibly causing the pot to burst and ruining it.

After wedging, if the clay is not to be used immediately it should be stored in airtight bins or polythene bags. It will then keep indefinitely and in time will develop a decidedly musty smell which is not altogether unpleasant. This is a sign that it is mature, and comes from bacterial action within the material.

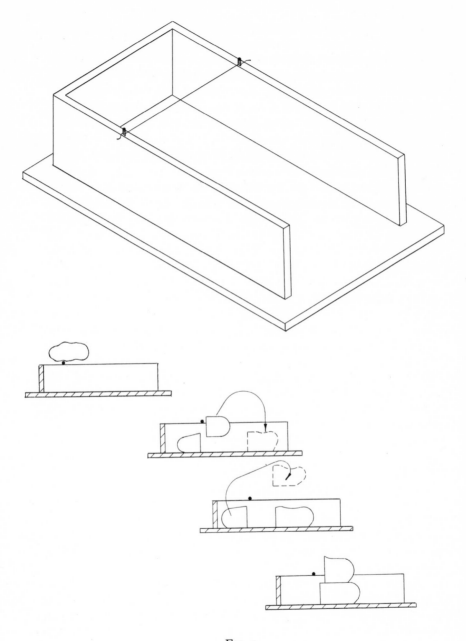

FIG. 5

The plaster sink may be used again and again to extract water provided it is given time to dry between each occasion. Soft clay and cuttings deposited in the scrap bucket during throwing and turning can be reclaimed in the same way and clay which is a little too wet for immediate use can have its water extracted either by leaving a sheet of it lying on the plaster for half an hour or so or by wedging and flinging the pieces down on to the plaster surface a few times.

A very simple wedging board is shown in figure 6. This consists of a cardboard or wooden box, any convenient container with an open top will do, which must be placed on a firm table. Put a piece of thick wood such as a baking or bread board in the bottom. The clay can be thrown down hard on to this without

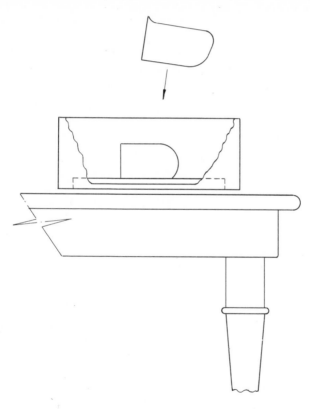

Fig. 6

fear of scatter towards surrounding furniture. If the surface of the board has a *Formica* or similar finish it will not tend to extract any more water.

Should the clay have been allowed to become too dry to work, it is quite easy to recover its customary plasticity in either of the following ways: spread a layer of the hard clay on a non-absorbent surface to a depth of about one inch. Now make a series of impressions with the thumb to within an inch of the bottom, each hollow should be spaced about $\frac{1}{2}$ an inch from the next. Pour roughly a thimbleful of water into each and leave for an hour. The walls of the impressions may crack but this does not matter. Pour away the surplus water, gather the clay into a ball and wedge in the usual way. Another method often used to soften clay is to cut it into thin slices each approximately $\frac{1}{8}$ of an inch thick. Sprinkle water on to each slice and leave to sink in for a little while, then reassemble. Finally, of course, thorough wedging must follow to regain uniformity.

Clay which is so dry that it cannot be cut with a wire should be crushed and left to soften with a little water in the bottom of a bucket.

3
WHAT YOU CAN DO WITH THE STUFF

Not all of us wish to go to the trouble of winning and refining our own clay body. There is always the risk that, after quite a lot of work, the end product will not be suitable for firing at all. Whilst, as has already been said, there is nothing quite so fascinating as being responsible for the product right from the preparation of the raw material to the fired piece, many potters obtain their body from one of the well known suppliers. Clay is cheap and is offered in a number of grades costing 2d to 5d per pound, depending upon quality and the amount ordered.

Much can be done without a wheel; in fact with such a medium there is no end to the possibilities which are instantly to hand, using practically no tools at all. Take a piece of red clay weighing about 2 oz. Form it into a ball by rolling it between the palms. Throw it down on to a piece of wood or a plate (figure 7). It will now have a flat base on which it can sit quite firmly during the next few minutes. Wet the first two fingers and thumb of the right hand and by gently squeezing and pulling draw one side of the lump into a point. This will be the nose of our first mouse. Keeping the fingers moist stroke his back into a curve. The ears are made by rolling a thin sausage of clay about $\frac{1}{4}$ of an inch in diameter under the fingers on a flat board. Cut off two discs each about $\frac{1}{16}$ of an inch thick. With the point of a penknife roughen the places where they are to be fixed. Prepare a little slurry by mixing some soft clay with water until it feels like melting butter. Use this *slip*, as it is called, as cement and press the ears firmly into position. After a few hours the clay mouse will be quite hard and can be prised off its base. If you wish to speed up the drying process a little, it can be warmed near a stove or radiator until firm, but there the forced drying should cease or it may crack. You should now be able to handle it without any risk of damage, and the time has come to scoop out some of its inside. This helps to let the steam escape during firing.

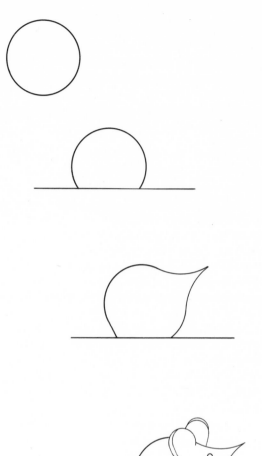

FIG. 7

Alternatively, one can make a number of blind holes in the underside with a twist drill, as is shown in figure 8. Pierce a hole to represent each eye: a knitting needle or match stick can be used for this, but a twist drill is best. Add a third hole at the stern which should go right through to one of the hollowed out parts. This will be used to take a leather bootlace after firing—the tail.

FIG. 8

The hedgehog and the piggy are made in a similar way (figure 8). The hedgehog has its surface scratched with a pin or any pointed instrument to represent bristles and the piggy may have a series of holes in his back so it can be used as a stand for cocktail sticks. One should remember that all clay contracts as it dries and again during the last stages of firing, and allowance must be made for this when cutting holes into which another article will have to fit. Many other animals can be modelled

FIG. 9

starting from very simple basic shapes. Some like the elephant, figure 9 (while still soft), usually have to be supported temporarily with cardboard props or even lumps of harder clay. The bigger the structure of the figure, the more important it is to remove as much clay as possible from the inside. Another hazard is the unequal contraction of one piece. Small, thin walls tend to dry more quickly than thick ones, so parts may crack and break off before the piece even reaches the kiln. The best safeguard is to keep any figure which is at all complicated in a damp wooden box covered with a lid. By watching progress, one can prolong the drying period and make it last a week. If it is going too fast, put some wet cloths in the box and close the lid. If too slowly, take the lid off for a while. It sounds very tedious but if you have a few sculptures which have taken hours to assemble it is worth the effort.

Slabwork entails the building of special pottery shapes from sheets of clay. An ordinary rolling-pin is perfectly satisfactory

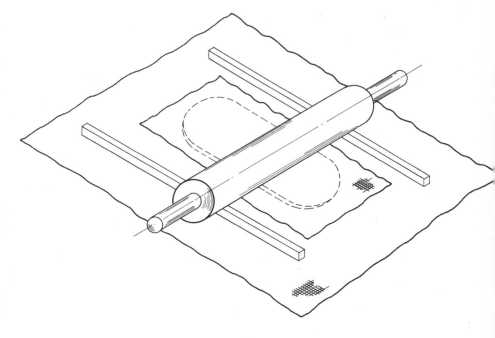

FIG. 10

for preparing the material: it is best to spread a cloth on the table first and insert a second one between the clay and the roller. This prevents sticking and also makes it easier to pick up the sheet of clay when it is ready. Two narrow guide laths about $\frac{1}{4}$ of an inch deep (or as required) may be used to keep the clay the same thickness throughout (figure 10).

In making a dish or any other article it is advisable for all the clay used to have come from the same wedged lump, so that it has an equal moisture content and all the parts will eventually contract by the same amount. When the various bits have been cut out, those which are not being assembled immediately should be covered with a damp cloth. When two surfaces are to be joined they should both be roughened and treated with a good coat of slurry. Where possible, sharp corners should be avoided as they are sources of weakness. They are the points where cracks start and after glazing they are the most vulnerable for flaking of the coating. All outside corners should be rounded off and the internal ones filled in with thin strips of rolled clay pressed into position to form a fillet (figure 11). Lute the surfaces together by gentle working with a wet cloth until all evidence of a join has completely disappeared.

Small trays and dishes can be formed on any existing shape which may be used as a pattern or template. Choose one over which you can spread a sheet of clay on the outside rather than attempting to use the inner surface as a mould. It is simpler to stretch the clay over something than to coax a sheet into a convex impression. If, on the other hand, you are simply taking a solid cast from a die or mould there is no problem. Repetition work of this sort savours of the factory and requires little or no skill. It is, however, creative to make one's own mould, and this can be done quite easily using plaster of Paris. A modern plastic scale pan makes an excellent former. Fill the inside with liquid plaster: it will not stick to a smooth surface and so will do no damage. If you are worried that it may stick or if the surface is at all rough you can paint the pan with a few layers of soft soap (obtainable from any chemist). As soon as the plaster has set, cast a stalk to support it by rolling some stiff paper into a cylinder and placing in the centre (figure 12). Make it watertight at the bottom by running in a few spoonfuls of half set plaster and then pour in the rest. When dry remove the mould pan and let the

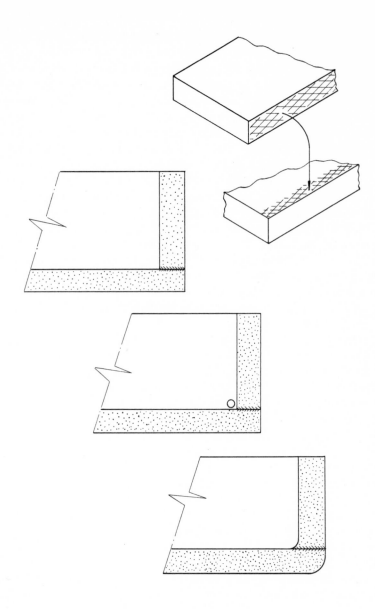

Fig. 11

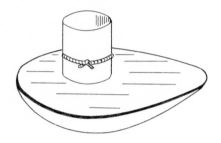

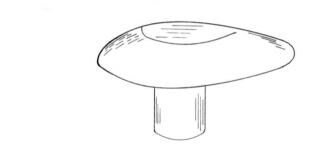

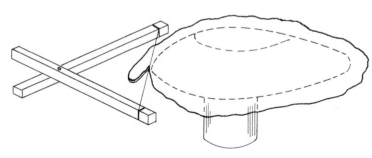

FIG. 12

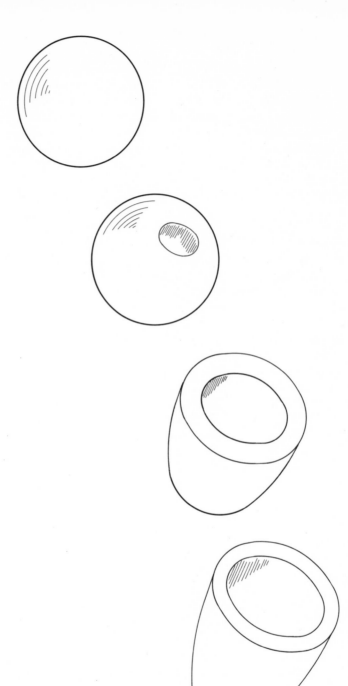

FIG. 13

plaster harden before use. Later, to make a clay dish using the mould, a rolled out sheet of clay is lifted on its cloth and smoothed round the contours of the plaster. The edges are trimmed by means of a piece of thin wire stretched across a catapult-shaped frame. It is possible to elaborate the mould a little by adding an embossed design to the inside of the tray before pouring in the plaster. This can be in clay: a leaf pattern for example, or just a coin would be unusual.

Reproductions of medals, small carvings and so on are made in the same way by first casting a 'negative'—the correct word in pottery is *intaglio*—in plaster and using this to leave an impression on a button of clay pressed into it. Later, colours can be added using one of the methods described in Chapter 5.

Perhaps one of the earliest practical uses of clay in any form was the vessel or container made by pinching a lump of brown body. To make one of these little pots, take a piece of clay weighing about 1 lb. and, after rounding it in the hands, press the thumb into the middle till it reaches to within about ¾ of an inch of the outside. Now moisten it and whilst turning the ball round in the left hand keep stroking the internal face with the thumb of the right. This action gradually thins the wall so that the pot tends to grow in diameter and height (figure 13). When finished, the clay should be about ⅜ of an inch thick and the vessel should look like rather more than half a coconut. Smooth the outside and trim the top by fixing a knife firmly in some convenient support and slowly rotating the pot so that the rough edges are cut away (figure 14). Round off the top lip with a damp cloth.

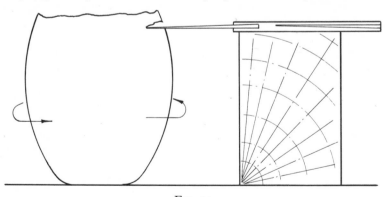

FIG. 14

Bigger pots can be made by the process known as *coiling*. This also is an ancient art but is now little practised commercially except in certain primitive regions. Having wedged a supply of clay prepare a number of long round ribbons using the following method. Fashion a sausage of clay about an inch in diameter and six inches long. Roll it on a smooth hard surface under the palms of the hands using only moderate pressure. Keep the fingers stretched straight and rigid. As the piece increases in length, the hands must run out to the sides to cover the extremities during each backward and forward stroke. The aim should be to produce a strip of clay with a uniform diameter for most of its length. Usually the coils will be about $\frac{3}{8}$ of an inch in diameter at the bottom of the pot and perhaps $\frac{1}{4}$ of an inch at the top near the rim. It is also a good plan to make a few much thinner strips in the same way which will be used later to fill in the grooves between the main coils. Keep all clay, which is not to be used immediately, covered with a damp cloth so as to retain the moisture. A large tile forms a useful surface on which to commence building your pot. It is not a bad plan to place a piece of paper on it first which allows the structure to contract as it dries, and may save it from cracking.

Now take one of the strips and form it into a spiral. This will be the base of the pot. Use the thinner pieces which you have just made to fill in the cracks and smooth all together with a flat wooden spatula so that eventually you have a disc. Roughen the top edge with a knife and commence to build up the wall in the same way. Lute each coil gently into the one below as you progress. When you come to join two lengths together, slit one and flatten the other so that they unite like a snake devouring the tail of a companion.

It is not easy to build a coiled pot, especially a tall one. Nevertheless it is an excellent exercise in the control of clay and some very beautiful examples of this art are regularly produced by students. If you have no wheel, coiling is a very satisfying substitute.

When finished the thickness of the wall of a coiled piece may be uniform, if it is a small one. Larger pots, however, will need to have the walls tapering from perhaps as much as $\frac{1}{2}$ an inch at the base to $\frac{1}{4}$ of an inch at the top. The inside and outside surfaces can be quite smooth or the individual coils may be left visible to

32

show how the pot was made which also gives a pleasing appearance.

A coiled pot can be decorated in the same variety of ways as one which has been thrown. Designs can be scratched on the surface; it can be carved, or coloured to make it gay and attractive. These processes are described in Chapter 5.

If the pot is to be turned into a jug, the lip can be formed in the following manner: support the rim at each side with the finger and thumb, then by a combined patting and stroking motion of the wet finger of the right hand, commence gradually to coax the wall into the appropriate shape (figure 15). Finish

FIG. 15

with a slight downward, cynical curl to the lip as this prevents drips when the jug is in use.

There is a time honoured way of making the handle. Take a lump of properly wedged clay and fashion it into the shape of a carrot. Hold the top in the left hand over a bucket of water with the point downwards. Keep continually wetting the right hand whilst lightly gripping and pulling in a stroking motion which soon lengthens the carrot into a strip (figure 16). When long enough, smartly turn the thick end the other way up and the strip will form a graceful curve of its own accord (figure 17). Secure the loose end temporarily against the side of the carrot and put away until leather hard. Later, when pot and handle are judged to have reached the same stage of drying, it is safe to fit them together. Once again, in this case, the surfaces are roughened and slurry applied to both. Finish by adding thin strips of

34

clay to blend the two parts so that they appear to flow into each other and lute with a wet cloth. Be sure to allow a piece with a handle to dry very slowly indeed. Keep it in a damp box so that the process is controlled and uniform. If there are signs of small cracks developing where the handle joins the body, close these carefully with the point of a wet penknife and if necessary press a little soft clay into the crevice. A handle which snaps in the middle is really a total loss and it is not worth trying to salvage it.

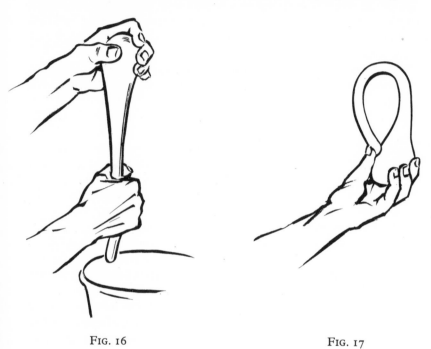

FIG. 16   FIG. 17

4
USING THE WHEEL

There are very few operations which look so simple yet which, in fact, are so difficult to master as throwing. Once learned, however, it is not easily forgotten and soon it becomes a skill which is, in itself, completely absorbing and satisfying. The process is almost as fascinating to watch as to perform. There are few who are not intrigued to see the craftsman create, in a few simple and graceful movements, a series of beautiful curves from a previously shapeless mass of clay: to see the pot rising as if by magic from the surface of the wheel, to watch it yield to the light touch of the fingers, and to change as it spins from something crude and meaningless to a bowl or vase, a thing of grace and purpose. Many who stand and admire the skill of the thrower long to be able to emulate him. Some have had the opportunity of trying at evening classes or the like. Others would dearly like to do so. It is perhaps not fully realised what a very wide gap indeed exists between the professional producing, frequently, a pot a minute and the performance of even the most accomplished amateur. Nevertheless whilst the industrial exponent is only interested in speed and accuracy he loses much in spontaneity. This can only be fostered by the true artist who is content with half a dozen pieces an hour. Each one of his is different, each in its own way tending to bear the imprint of his personality.

There is no easy way to learn to throw. One can only study certain basic principles, apply them to the best of one's ability and then settle down to practise, not for a few hours, but for days, for weeks. Only by constant experience, by continuous contact with clay in all its moods, by controlling and experimenting with the wheel, can one hope eventually to achieve a measure of perfection. There is no short cut.

With that rather gloomy introduction let us see if we can follow the steps in making a simple pot. The clay which is to be used for throwing must be perfectly mixed. The slightest unevenness in texture will only introduce hazards which surely lead to frustration and disaster. Meticulous care in wedging is therefore absolutely essential and just before starting there are many who give the lump to be used a few final cuts and thumps to be on the safe side.

The wheel itself should be cleaned: it must not be perfectly dry, just very slightly moist if the clay is to stick to it efficiently. Have the lump in the form of a ball weighing about 1 lb. and throw it down hard, aiming for the centre of the disc. If it should land out of position, as it is very likely to do, carefully squeeze it over until it finishes approximately in the middle. Pat it gently until it is nearly circular. Study the photographs; they will tell you more than can be described in print.

Splash on plenty of water, wet the hands and set the wheel spinning at full speed. It should turn anti-clockwise seen from above. Rest the elbows or forearms on the nearest firm support afforded by the wheel framework and then place the palms of the hands on each side of the spinning mass. The clay will almost certainly be wobbling outrageously, even though when still it seemed central, and the hands of the beginners will move with it. The clay is working its will on you whereas it should be the other way round. You must start immediately to gain mastery of the situation. You must aim to mould the clay so that your hands remain stationary, so that no matter how fast the wheel turns they appear perfectly still. When this stage is reached the lump will be round and it will occupy the exact centre of the wheelhead. This centering operation is usually thought to be one of the most difficult tasks for the beginner but until it can be done reasonably quickly it is useless to proceed further. To start the process of centering place the left hand so that the fingers are together and the palm vertical and at right angles to the top of the wheel. The palm should be just in contact with the side of the clay. Now put the right hand on top of the lump, again with the fingers joined and the thumb down one side. If the piece of clay is small there is no harm in the side of the right hand, that is the edge of the first finger, touching the palm of the left (figure 18).

With the wheel at full speed press the left hand horizontally towards the centre, if necessary using whatever leverage is available from the arm rest. This will tend to make the disc circular and to thicken it, so the right hand must lift slightly as

37

the clay rises. Now reverse the action by pressing down with the right hand. This will flatten the top and start to make the disc thinner. The palm of the left hand should resist somewhat, continuing to press inwards towards the centre but at the same time grudgingly permit the disc to increase in diameter. The clay should be worked in this way a few times. If it feels at all rough then more drastic kneading is necessary. Using plenty of water grasp it at both sides with the two hands and squeeze it as it spins which will cause it to rise into a cone. Press this down again

FIG. 18

with the palm of the right hand whilst guiding it with the left and repeat. When satisfied that the material is indeed in perfect condition, finish with one more downward pressure with the right palm and contain the expansion of the disc as before with the left. The hands should now be motionless with the clay spinning underneath. Take the hands away very slowly. A good rule is never to have any contact with the clay unless it is turning, and never stop the wheel until both hands are disengaged. If it still persists in wobbling at the end of the process, repeat it.

Having formed a perfect disc the creation of the shape of the pot can commence. The first step is the cutting of a hole in the centre. Splash more water on to the clay and have the hands wet. Place the right hand round the edge of the wheelhead if it is small enough, otherwise round the disc itself, and let the thumb reach over towards the centre. Have the other hand in contact

38

with the opposite edge. Press the right thumb down in the middle whilst guiding and steadying it with pressure from the left thumb. Allow the clay to flow smoothly out of the way as the ball of the thumb advances downwards. This is fundamental to all work on the wheel and the expert gets to know how fast he can move without risk of losing concentricity. If the hole, when finished, proves to be even slightly out of centre it is better to start all over again. Only the very experienced potter would be able to retrieve such a situation so it is really a waste of time for the beginner to try. The thumb should continue to within

FIG. 19

about $\frac{1}{2}$ an inch of the wheelhead. One learns to judge this distance but at first there is no harm in stopping the wheel and pushing a needle through the bottom to measure the remaining thickness of clay. The tiny mark so made soon knits together again and will leave no trace. This is almost the only movement which may be carried out safely with the wheel stationary.

The central hole must now be made larger to form a very thick low dish. With the recess just formed full of water, wet the hands and again place the right thumb inside. The fingers should be round the outer wall gently guiding it but applying no pressure. Now steadily swing the right thumb outwards increasing the size of the opening (figure 19). The movement must be smooth, allowing plenty of time for the clay to flow out of the

39

way. Any sudden action or unnecessary force may cause the work to move off centre. The wheel should be running fairly fast so that a zone in contact with the thumb rotates a number of times for the slightest shift in the position of the hands. The fingers should be still positioned partially curled round the outside but exerting no pressure. Once again permit the material to flow naturally rather than to force it. Use plenty of water. If the pressure is quite steady and the action perfectly smooth, you should finish with a flat disc surrounded by a rim about 1 inch high and ¾ of an inch thick.

At this stage it is wise for the beginner to wipe the hands clean of slurry before going any further. The basis of practically every thrown pot, except of course a dish, is the plain cylinder of clay which must now be formed. It is usually made in about three stages. The unskilled worker may take more. If, however, the process is too protracted the clay absorbs so much water that it becomes too soft and may collapse. This is one of the reasons why throwing presents the learner with so many problems. To be successful, the pot must be made quickly. This ensures that, although copious supplies of water may be employed as a lubricant, it remains on the surface and does not have time to penetrate into the interior and so weaken the clay being handled. The beginner tends to be overcautious, raising the cylinder only a fraction of an inch or so at every attempt. The longer the struggle persists the less chance there is of a favourable outcome. The secret is to know the properties of the clay and the liberties which can be taken with it. One works just fast enough to avoid distortion. Place the elbows on firm supports at the sides of the wheel, if available. In the case of the Mini-wheel the motor shelf will do quite well. Have the hands very wet, put the thumbs together inside the disc with the fingers pointing downwards outside it. Where the speed of the wheel can be varied the clay may now be running a little slower than before. Very gently squeeze the thumbs towards the fingers, trapping the rim at the point where it is joined to the base. In figure 20 a cross-section of the disc is shown, so that the shape of the wall at this stage may be clearly understood. Be sure to allow the clay to flow out of the way. The effect will be to undercut the rim and to create a bulge above the ball of the thumb. Try to judge the thickness of the wall: it should not be less than ½ an inch at this stage and five-

40

eighths of an inch would be acceptable. If all has gone well the clay will still be spinning centrally, so continue as follows. Keep the tips of the fingers pointing downwards and without relaxing the squeeze begin slowly to raise both hands vertically. As they rise, the thumbs should be preceded by the bulge of clay which is progressively paid out to become the side of a squat cylinder. Repeat the process and with care it should be possible to double the height of the wall. If there is any tendency for the clay to drag or feel rough in places, more water must be used to make it slippy. For the third lift it may be found that the wall is now too tall to be reached at the bottom by the fingers and thumb of the same hand, so a different technique must be adopted. Up to this

FIG. 20

point it is relatively easy to control the distance between the thumb and fingers and so determine the thickness of the clay. However, as the height of the cylinder increases, one has to work with the left hand inside and the right hand outside. One also needs a firm pad against which to press the spinning clay. The extended fingers of the left hand are placed inside and the thumb is used to form a bridge across to the right hand and the pad on the outside against which the wall is pressed is made by the crooked first finger (figure 21). This must be practised until the position can be adopted automatically. It is fundamental, and so, if further progress is to be made, has to be mastered. By way of further explanation, figure 21A shows the bent first finger, but turned outwards away from the cylinder so that you can see its shape. The next increase in height, then, is the result of pressing outwards at the bottom of the wall with the fingers of the left hand and resisting with the crooked first finger of the right on the outside whilst again raising the forearms. The thickness can be controlled quite well using the bridge of the left thumb to maintain uniformity. The cylinder ought now to taper from between $\frac{1}{2}$ an inch and three-eighths of an inch at the bottom to roughly $\frac{1}{4}$ of an inch at the top. Later with heavier lumps of clay the cylinder will be too tall even for this method, in which case the two hands have to work entirely independently which is a little more difficult. This final step in forming the cylinder is explained in figure 22.

When generating the cylinder, by whichever of the three

FIG. 21   FIG. 21A

FIG. 22

means described, it should always be remembered that the speed of the wheel must be such that two or three revolutions are made every time the bulge travels upwards a distance equivalent to its own thickness. In fact the more turns the better. However, if it spins too fast the clay will be thrown outwards by centrifugal force. This tendency develops mainly at the top. The squeezing of the clay also causes the wall to decrease in thickness and for the cylinder to become larger in diameter. This effect can be corrected from time to time as it develops by *collaring*. To do this the hands are wetted and they are then made to encircle the clay near the base as it spins. Both are now slowly raised and as they progress towards the rim the diameter is reduced. The process may have to be repeated once or twice and much care is needed. Do not attempt to make too big a change at one pass. To do so would be to risk creasing the wall and once this happens the fault is difficult to correct. The thinner the clay the more caution must be employed. This is easy to understand if it is remembered that in collaring one is really applying pressure to the opposite ends of a thin strip of soft material in an effort to shorten and thicken it. The natural tendency would be for the strip to kink rather than for it to grow fatter. By raising the hands as well as squeezing the cylinder one gives the clay the opportunity to flow upwards and so, to some extent at least, the chance of buckling is lessened. The act of collaring does three things. It makes the wall thicker, it reduces the diameter and it creates a taller shape.

If the cylinder has buckled or formed ripples (usually spiral in shape) it can sometimes be corrected. Much depends upon how bad the trouble has become. Ripples are due to weakness in the wall either because it is too thin or because the clay has been collared too violently. Try and strengthen the thin part by gently bringing up more material from the zone at the base and so gradually build up the part which is tending to collapse. As the fingers travel upwards towards the ripple zone the pressure should be relaxed and this will leave a thicker layer of clay where it is needed. Ripples which have formed from too rapid collaring can often be smoothed away by pressure with the fingers from inside, so reversing the process and increasing the diameter locally temporarily. The next stage is to try and build up the wall thickness as described above and only after this should collaring be resumed, rather more cautiously.

Once the required height has been reached, if not before, all surplus water must be removed from the inside while the wheel is turning. To do this use a sponge tied to a piece of stick; there must be no puddle left at the bottom. Continue to wring out the sponge and apply again and again to the bottom of the pot until it ceases to shine, so you know that it is no wetter than the rest of the body (figure 23).

Assuming the thrower has raised, say, a 5-inch cylinder without mishap and provided it is reasonably true, the shape of

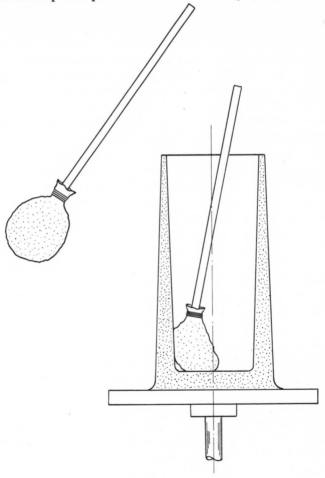

FIG. 23

the pot can now be formed. The expert frequently creates this in a few seconds with a single flowing movement starting at the base and finishing with the rim. Only minor adjustments follow. By so doing he is certain to generate perfectly balanced curves and this is the ultimate achievement. Such immediate success is almost certain to elude the beginner except, perhaps, with very small pieces. The extended fingers of the left hand should be positioned inside at the base and the crooked first finger of the right hand immediately opposite outside. The two hands must move in unison as the arms are raised. To bulge outwards, pressure from within is applied and controlled from without. To turn the clay towards the centre the opposite action is required. To begin with, one should be content to develop the pot in stages, stopping at intervals to check and carefully correct where necessary. This detailed adjustment can often be done just with a single wet finger. The rings on the surface which result are no detriment at all and are, in fact, attractive as they indicate that the article has indeed been hand thrown and is not mass produced. If, on the other hand, a smooth finish is preferred this can be rendered with the side of the finger or with what are called *ribbing* tools. These are metal shapes with curves which can be held against the side of a piece as it rotates. They are not intended to impart form but only as devices to give the final finish. When making a simple plant pot, a steel ruler or straight edge will perform this function (figure 24). It must be wetted and gripped very firmly by both hands whilst being advanced extremely slowly against the clay to avoid a sudden snatch which, at the best, would leave a deep mark and, at the worst, completely wreck the work. A slightly damp sponge held against the piece and slowly raised from base to rim leaves a pleasing finished surface.

Sometimes the rim may be uneven in which case it can be trimmed with a sharp spike or a needle (stuck in a cork to make it easier to grip). Set the wheel turning, and with the first finger of the left hand just brushing the inside at the point to be cut off (this should be about an eighth of an inch beneath the lowest dip in the edge), advance the needle slowly from the outside with the right hand (figure 25), resting the elbow on a firm support to keep it steady. When the point breaks through, it is possible to lift both hands smartly and without stopping the wheel to pick up the ring of clay just severed. This is quite an impressive little

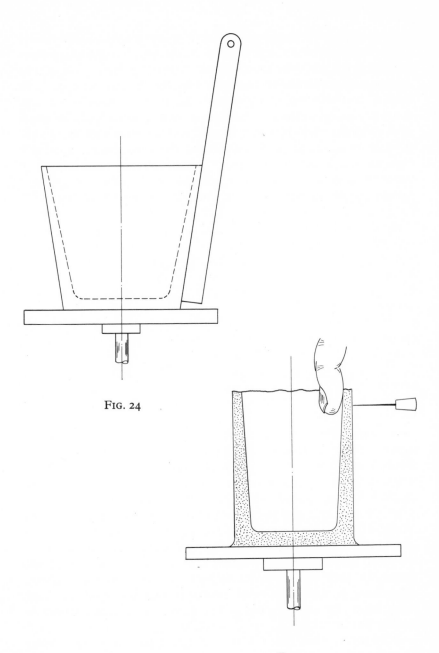

FIG. 24

FIG. 25

movement which is not too difficult to accomplish. A perfectly centred and thrown pot should need no trimming at all, but there are times when it is necessary even for the experienced worker to carry out this remedial measure and the learner may, at first, have to do it every time. If you fail to disengage the ribbon of clay with the wheel turning there is no need to panic. Stop the wheel and carefully pick off the severed pieces with the needle point. Should a length fall inside the pot and defy all efforts at picking it out, leave it alone. Later when the piece dries it will be easy to remove it; in fact it may crack and fall away by itself. Any slight roughness of the surface can be scratched off with a knife blade

FIG. 26

when the chalk hard stage is reached. Trimming the rim usually leaves a sharp corner at the top which is undesirable because it looks untidy and is a source of possible trouble later, when in the kiln, so it should be rounded off as follows. Take a piece of the softest chamois leather about 2 inches square, wet it so that it feels smooth and pliable and with the wheel running at medium speed allow the rim to nestle in a loop of the leather held between the finger and thumb of the right hand as is shown in figure 26. Keep the material very moist; if it is too dry it will snatch and bend the clay out of shape. Now is the time to mop up any remaining water which may have splashed inside. To be very meticulous, dry the sponge on a duster before applying it to collect the last traces.

The base of the pot still looks rather untidy as there is likely to be surplus clay near the wheelhead, this should now be cut

47

away. For this operation one uses a turning tool. These can be bought but, in fact, the best are home made and are not at all difficult to manufacture. Examples of such tools are shown in figure 27. They are all simply bent pieces of steel strip sharpened

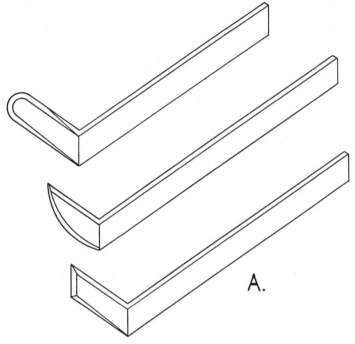

A.

FIG. 27

with a file. There should be no attempt to trim the whole of the pot but merely to remove unwanted material which tends to accumulate near the base during the process of throwing. Work downwards starting from a point about an inch from the wheel.

FIG. 28

When the excess has been cut away the outline should blend with the shape of the rest of the piece (figure 28). The tool marks should be obliterated either with the finger or by trailing a damp sponge against the clay.

In removing the pot from the wheel it may seem an almost insuperable problem not to damage the work in transit. It is impressive to watch the expert cut the base with a wire and then deftly lift it off by gripping the sides with his hands. One hesitates to suggest to the beginner that he should do it this way, as disaster after much patient labour would be heartbreaking. However, there is another method which is reasonably simple. The wire or nylon is used to sever and then a flexible steel shim or very wide pallet knife known as a *pot lifter* is pressed underneath. There is risk of some distortion as the base bends during removal but this can be easily corrected later. If the pot is still oval, even after careful manoeuvring of the bat on which it is placed, leave it alone until it dries to the leather hard stage and then gently correct it by inserting a tumbler or basin of suitable size. Twist it against the inside and this will cause the rim to become perfectly round once more. For the beginner the following way to remove a pot is perhaps the simplest and safest. Have ready one or two bats cut as shown in figure 29 to fit the wheel. Hardboard, plywood or better still one of the modern plastic lino tiles will do. Splash some water on to the wheelhead and keeping the wire pressed hard down on to the metal draw it forward under the pot (figure 30). The first time it may cut the clay quite cleanly leaving the piece itself exactly where it was. The wetter the clay the more likely this is to happen. Wet the wheel again and cut a second time. Usually either the pot will tend to travel with the wire or there may be just a slight movement so that it is displaced by about an eighth of an inch. If the piece slides along towards the edge of the wheel astride the wire, make the wire into a loop, hold it in the right hand, and give a sharp tug. It should come away and leave the pot behind. If done properly there is no need to worry about the pot jerking forward over the edge; its own inertia will ensure that it stays still. However, as a safeguard for the first attempt, there is no harm in placing a restraining finger in the way. If, however, after passing the wire three times underneath, the pot remains stubbornly in the middle there is a certain way of shifting it. Once more use plenty of water. Draw

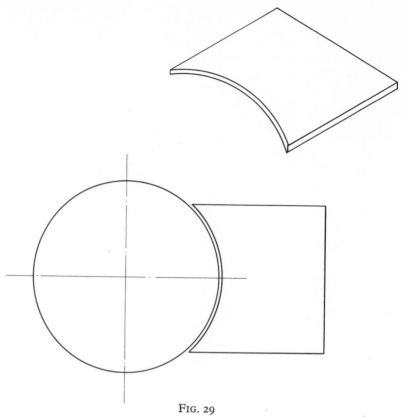

FIG. 29

FIG. 30

the wire underneath but stop halfway. Once again hold the two ends together leaving a loop under the base (figure 31). Slowly pull with the right hand whilst at the same time pushing the other side with the edge of the finger laid flat on the wheel. It

FIG. 31

should now float off on to a film of water and can be coaxed towards the edge with the very lightest of force. Wet the surface of the bat and place it against the wheel with its top exactly level. The piece can now be eased smoothly on to it, as in figure 32,

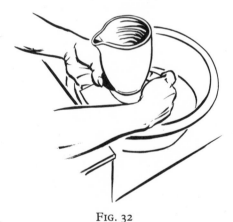

FIG. 32

and so lifted safely away and put somewhere to dry. As it does so, it will stick to the bat and if left in this state the bottom will almost certainly crack. The larger the diameter of the base the greater is the risk. Therefore, as soon as the clay is

51

hard enough to be handled it should be cut off or somehow dis-engaged and be left to finish drying out on a piece of paper. If the bat is semi-flexible (one made from a thin *Vinyl* tile is reasonably so), it is easy to peel it away from the base supporting the pot in the cupped hand as it is freed. After releasing it from the bat leave the pot on a piece of paper which will not interfere with its shrinkage. A rigid bat is not so simple to separate from a pot and resort may have to be made to the wire to cut through the clay. If left too long this may prove quite a struggle. In a crisis try a flexible pot lifter if available or, lacking one of these, cut through with a hacksaw blade. Failure to free the piece will, unless it is very small, ultimately risk its loss, so every effort must be made to achieve disengagement. Should a crack have already developed, provided the clay is still leather hard and flexible, it can be closed up by pressure and if necessary with a little soft clay pushed inside. Once the pot has dried to the chalk hard stage (by which time it has usually released itself anyway) it is more difficult to fill a crack successfully.

No pot can be considered finished until it has been given a *footring* which makes it stand properly without rocking on its base. It is true that many studio potters omit this refinement nowadays and obtain a degree of embellishment and undercutting with a twisted wire when severing the pot from the wheelhead, but there is nothing quite the same as a well proportioned ring. Examples are shown in figure 33, and are made as follows. As soon as the piece is safe to handle and is rigid enough to stand upside down on its rim it is remounted on the wheel. This may present some difficulties if the pot is a tall one and suggestions for handling these will be made later. For an average simple shape, the following procedure is recommended. Take about 8 oz. of clay and throw it as hard as possible on to the centre of the wheel. Spread it manually over the surface until it is roughly even. Whilst rotating the wheel quite fast use a strip of steel or wood to level it so that there is a carpet of clay about $\frac{1}{4}$ of an inch thick, at least as big in diameter as the rim of the pot (figure 34). Place the pot bottom up as near to the middle as can be judged by the eye (figure 35). Keep spinning the wheel a few turns at a time and adjusting the position until it runs perfectly true. It is useful to have a firm rest of some sort, for instance a piece of wood across the sides of the wheel casing, on which to support

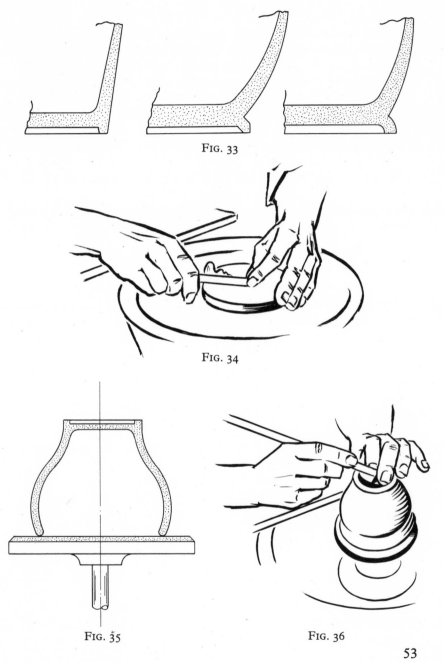

FIG. 33

FIG. 34

FIG. 35

FIG. 36

the hand guiding the tool. Place the first two fingers of the left hand on the top of the pot, see figure 36. This will steady the pot as it rotates, by keeping it pressed down on to the coating of clay, and will avoid any risk of dislodgement during the next operation. A tool shaped as shown in figure 27A can be used to do most of the work but if a more intricate footring is required one or two

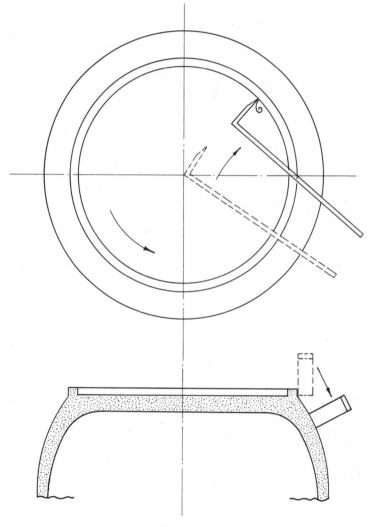

FIG. 37

alternatives may be needed. It must be sharp; if so, and providing the clay is in the right state, the material cut away should fall in long spirals. If it sticks to the metal it is too wet, if it flakes or powders, too dry. Start in the centre and create a flat circle into which the fingers of the left hand will naturally fall thus making the task of keeping the pot in position easier. Work out towards the edge, never forcing the tool, always letting it cut its way forward as it progresses steadily (figure 37). The surface should be left smooth and even. If the tool starts to vibrate so that a knurled effect is produced, this is a sign either that it is blunt, or that the point from which it is being supported is not sufficiently rigid. Bring the wood on which the hands rest as near as possible to the work and begin again starting with very light cuts until all the roughened part has been removed.

If the pot is a little too narrow at the top to be stable when mounted in the way described above, wads of clay can be added at the sides to give support (figure 38). They will, of course, be softer than the pot to be turned, so will subsequently come away quite easily without leaving a mark.

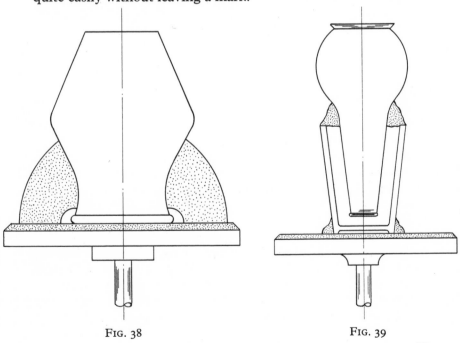

FIG. 38   FIG. 39

59

A very long necked tall vessel is always a problem when the footring has to be made. In this case it is helpful to find a jar or some such container into which the neck can be inserted (figure 39). The jar is then mounted on the clay carpet on the wheel, centred and given additional security by added lumps of clay round the outside. Further wads round the top will grip the piece itself so that it is safe to work on the base.

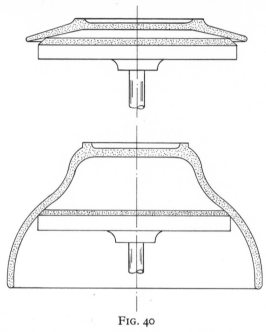

FIG. 40

To cut the footring on a large bowl or plate, the wheelhead has to be coated as before but this time the carpet must extend right up to the edge and the bowl may overlap it as shown in figure 40. There is a tendency, as the piece dries, for the underside to become convex and if the ring is not sufficiently deep the pot will rest on this *belly* after firing, and this is undesirable. Enough clay must therefore be removed to allow for the centre part bowing by taking a little more away than would appear necessary at this stage. The higher the biscuit temperature the greater the chance that the centre will drop. In the case of a large bowl the trouble can be counteracted, somewhat, by supporting the middle in the kiln as seen in figure 41. The thickness of the bottom can be

60

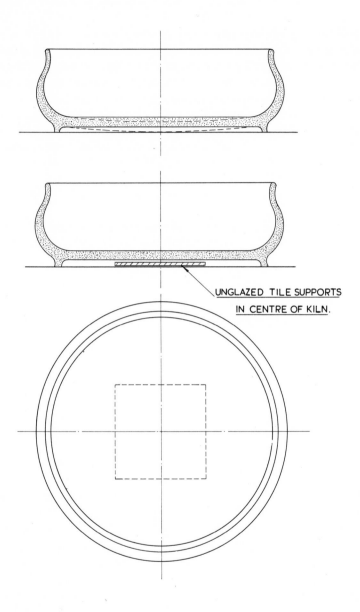

UNGLAZED TILE SUPPORTS
IN CENTRE OF KILN.

FIG. 41

judged by lightly tapping with the turning tool. A dull sound means it is safe to go on, a higher pitch gives warning that the wall is becoming perilously thin. In the case of a bowl, the bottom should never be less than the average thickness of the sides. Where a plate is being turned, never less than the rim.

There are many special shapes which can be thrown on the wheel. One of the most interesting of these is a tall narrow vase such as is frequently used for a single rose. In spite of the apparent problem of reaching the inside, it is not too difficult to make, provided the clay is properly prepared. The cylinder may be thrown exactly as has been described or it may be given an initial taper which is an advantage, the bottom being made a little larger than the top (figure 42). It is easier to create the bulge near the base if the sponge tied to the stick, normally used for mopping up surplus water, is applied to the inside (figure 43).

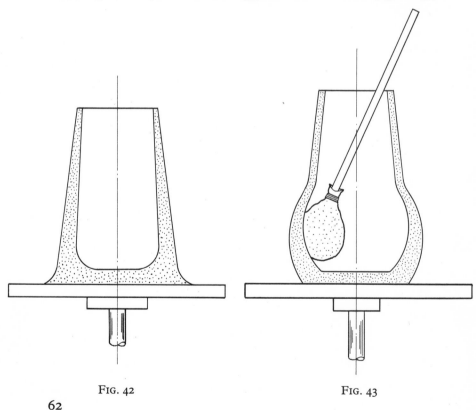

FIG. 42   FIG. 43

62

The right hand holding the stick applies outward pressure to the sponge at the end of it and the shape is controlled by an opposite force exerted inwards by the left hand pressed against the outside of the clay as it spins. When the lower part has been

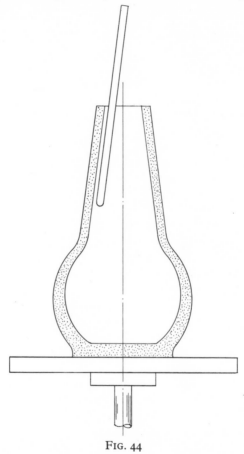

Fig. 44

formed it is time to remove any water which has collected inside, as once the neck has been closed-in this will no longer be possible. The diameter above the bulge is reduced by cautious external collaring, a little at each pass of the hands as they travel upwards towards the rim. The walls will tend to become thicker and slightly taller so this effect has to be cancelled from time to time pulling the cylinder thinner and higher. When working on a narrow neck it is very easy to lose concentricity or to promote ripples on the wall so only the very lightest pressure is necessary. The nearer to the top one is working and the longer the neck the greater the risk. The final shaping can often be conveniently accomplished by inserting a wet stick (which, of course, must be round) which can be used as a former against which to trap gently the rotating cylinder (figure 44). Before cutting from the wheel, it is usually necessary to trim the bottom with a turning tool.

When throwing a bowl, a plate or a large pot the procedure is somewhat different. In this case there is a considerable risk of destroying the piece when taking it off the wheel, and although this hazard may cause little concern to the professional, it is sometimes quite a worry to the beginner. The simplest solution is to mount a removable disc on the wheel which can be detached as soon as the process is completed. It is called a *bat*. Some wheels can be arranged to take special plaster discs prepared and suitably recessed to make them fit exactly on to the wheelhead but it is assumed in this book that no such aids exist and that the potter must make his own preparations. Have a circle of ¼-inch marine plywood cut about 1½ inches larger in diameter than the wheel itself. Fix three or four guides to the underside using pieces of timber ½ an inch by ½ an inch, as shown in figure 45, so that it is located exactly on the centre of the wheel without any clearance. Brass screws or one of the modern *Epoxy* self-curing resins can be used to fix the guides. Coat the wheelhead with a layer of soft clay about ¼ of an inch thick and scrape the surface quite smooth with a steel flat. This time make certain to take a little more out of the centre than at the edge so that the surface is slightly concave. This ensures that the outside part of the clay disc is in contact with the wood (figure 46) and it is at the larger diameter that the greatest driving force can be exerted. If only the central part were in contact, not only would the disc tend to rock but it would quickly start to slip as soon as any pressure was applied during centering. Now dampen the underside of the disc and press it down hard on to the clay. A smart, downward blow with the side of the fist will key the surfaces securely together. It is surprising how much torque can be transmitted in this way, yet it is still quite easy to disconnect the wooden bat by inserting a knife between it and the wheel and twisting. The great advantage of this system is that, having thrown the piece, it can be removed complete with its wooden base without fear of damage. Once again, however, care is needed to prevent cracking during drying. To avoid this, cut

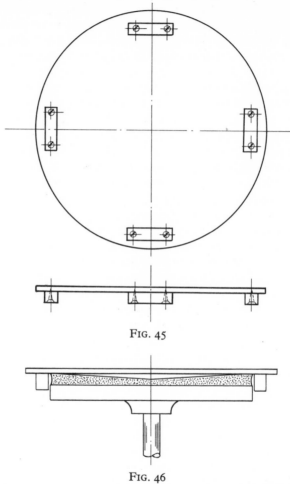

FIG. 45

FIG. 46

through the clay with the wire immediately after throwing and once or twice again before the pot gets hard. As soon as it can be safely lifted off the bat, place it on paper so that no harm will be done when the pot contracts.

To throw a bowl the actions are very similar to those described

66

above, except that the initial disc is larger in diameter and thicker according to the size of pot intended. If the bowl is to be comparatively high then a squat cylinder is formed in the usual way and the actions are exactly as already described. If the piece is to be shallow, on the other hand, a somewhat modified technique is required. After centering the disc, run the wheel a little slower and place the four fingers of the left hand down on the surface with the tip of the middle finger near the middle of the clay. Put the right hand near the edge of the disc with the fingers curled but space left between the thumb and the first finger to grip and guide the rim of the bowl as it forms. The rim begins to rise when the fingers of the left hand press down on the centre of the disc squeezing a ridge of clay out towards the edge. The thumb of the right hand receives the ridge and begins to build it higher by trapping it against the curved first finger. The height is controlled and the top of the rim made uniform by pressure downwards of the right hand just behind the part where the thumb joins the palm. Although this may sound rather complicated, in practice the process is quickly learned. The series of photographs show the actions much better than words can describe them. A bowl is far easier to produce than a tall pot. The larger the diameter the slower must the wheel turn. If it runs too fast the result will be a plate and not a very good one at that! Once this disaster happens there is no way of correcting the shape. When the bowl is nearing completion the final moulding of the rim may be done with the two first fingers working from opposite sides, using the left thumb as a bridge between the two hands.

A dish is also best thrown on a bat. No cylinder is made. The first step is to centre a flat disc of large diameter. The fingers are used as before to press down in the middle and are then drawn towards the edge preceded by a ridge of clay which gradually increases the diameter at each trip. A slight camber must be preserved, forming the hollow of the dish; this gives support without which the rim will collapse (figure 47). The edge can be thinned and smoothed between finger and thumb before the leather is applied to round off the corners. The centre of the plate must be dried as soon as possible with the sponge and this can also be used to flatten the middle and leave it reasonably even.

67

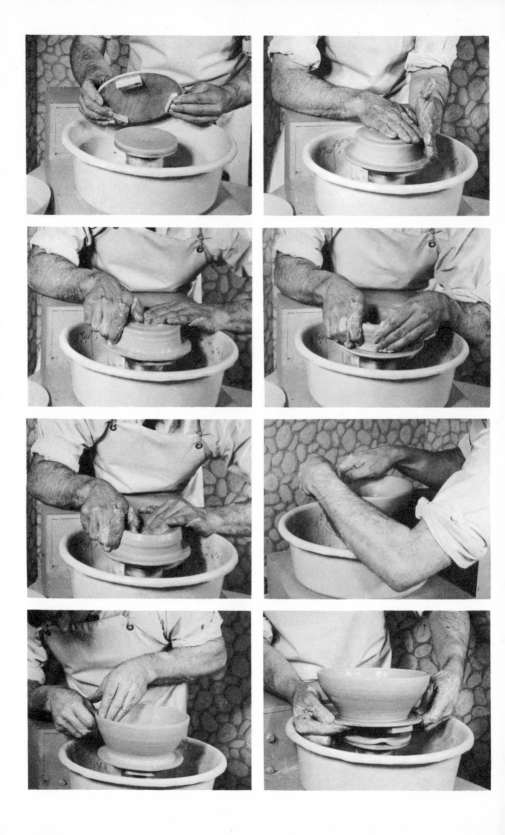

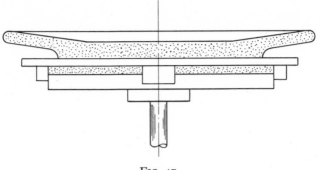

FIG. 47

A posy bowl is quite easy to throw on a bat, but this time, when the thumb is first introduced, immediately after centering, it is allowed to go right down to the wood. When the hole thus formed is enlarged the effect is to produce a thick ring of clay. The next step is to make a groove using the thumb again but stopping short of the bat by about ½ an inch. This leaves us with two concentric walls (figure 48), which are now treated in the usual way one at a time. No footring is necessary with this design but after partial drying it is customary to turn the bottom quite smooth and to radius the corners.

There is little more to add by way of advice to those who wish to work on the wheel. Remember always that the condition of the clay itself is of paramount importance. If it is only partially wedged there is little chance of centering properly, much less of throwing a pot successfully. The slightest unevenness of texture is instantly noticeable. Perfectly prepared body should feel silky smooth as it spins beneath the hands. It should not drag. Once the disc has been centred no adjustment whatever should be made with the wheel stopped. It must always be turning when in contact with the hands. It should start before the hands approach and stop after they leave. There is only one exception to this golden rule. That is when an air bubble, a splinter of wood or other foreign matter has been felt. In the case of the bubble, stop the wheel and puncture the thin skin by inserting a needle and tearing the surface. Gently fill in the depression so formed with soft clay of about the same degree of wetness as the rest and carefully smooth over the blemish. Restart the wheel and work on that spot with the finger up and down a few times.

69

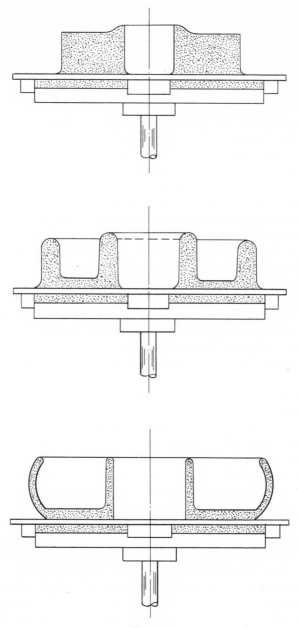

Fig. 48

With a little patience it is usually possible in this way to save a pot which would otherwise have been scrapped. Where a small foreign body has been detected this must also have immediate attention. Even the tiniest piece of grit or metal must be extracted if at all possible. Fortunately the fingers are so sensitive that they can often feel particles embedded in the clay which the eye has the greatest difficulty in seeing. Here again, stop the wheel and remove these with the needle. Then the cut must be made good with a little clay flattened into the hole.

Where possible try and match the speed of the wheel to the work. Reserve the high speeds for centering and small pots. As the pot grows larger in diameter the wheel must run more slowly.

Aim to make a pot quickly and mop all water from the interior at the earliest opportunity, while at the same time giving the material time to flow into position without too much pressure having to be applied.

A small piece, say 3 inches or 4 inches high, can be thrown from clay which is quite wet. One 6 inches or 9 inches in height needs a much drier body or the cylinder will tend to settle as fast as it is pulled upwards. Drier clay requires more force to centre it and, in fact, when you are working with lumps of 3 lb. and more you will find that considerable pressure is necessary to form the disc.

Pieces much larger than this may have to have the clay treated with what is called *grog* to give support and so stiffen the walls (grog is finely ground biscuit which has the same firing properties as the body with which it is mixed).

Practice making cylinders which spin true. Cut each one longitudinally with a wire and see whether the walls are of even thickness and have a uniform taper. It does not matter how many have to be scrapped; they all go in the bucket and the clay will be used again. In the end you will be able to make a cylinder of a given size in a few seconds, without hesitation, with no ragged rim and no wobble. Then, and only then, can you expect to be able to create really interesting and exciting shapes on the potter's wheel. To these there is no limit. The challenge is there; the opportunity is yours.

5
DECORATION

There is practically no limit to the forms of decoration which can be applied to pottery. It would be a large tome indeed which made pretence at covering them all. This chapter, therefore, will concentrate on a few of the more obvious effects which may be produced with little or no natural artistic gift or training. It is hoped that this will lead to better techniques and perhaps a quest for further information which can be acquired from more advanced books on this fascinating subject.

Although colours are useful, and greatly enhance the scope and the appeal of pottery, much can be done without them. For example, an orange stick or a kitchen fork will scratch interesting patterns on unfired clay and this form of decoration, carried out with primitive tools, was common thousands of years ago. Filigree work round a thrown pot can be cut at the leather hard stage with a sharp knife or one of those useful little *Xacto* tools obtainable in most 'do-it-yourself' shops (figures 49 and 50). For those who are interested in modern concepts of art, opportunities arise to build all sorts of exciting shapes in three dimensions, either from simple thrown cylinders or, better still, from the many other more sophisticated shapes produced by the wheel. All that is needed is a sharp cutter and a creative mind.

Leaves or other patterns can be carved out of thin sheets of clay and stuck to the outside of pots with a little slurry. Make sure however that the clays come from the same source as the pot and that they are at the same stage of drying or they will break away due to unequal water content.

A simple design can be impressed using a *Meccano* gear or a wheel from an old clock. Try making ringlets on the surface with the sharp end of the ferrule which holds the little rubber on some lead pencils (figure 51).

When making a dish from a mould, put a piece of coarse cloth between the clay and the plaster former used to impart the shape.

72

The pattern will be faithfully reproduced and is frequently more pleasing than a smooth surface. Try different cloth weaves to vary the embossed pattern.

FIG. 49

FIG. 50

FIG. 51

There are many other simple ideas which occur to every potter and the ones which are original are especially rewarding.

Pottery pigments are sold by many well known stockists in the form of powders or liquids which, generally speaking, are compounds of one metal or another. Ordinary colouring materials are not generally suitable as only chemicals which are capable of

73

withstanding the high temperatures involved in firing can be used. Even some of these have to be fired in special ways in order to yield some of the more troublesome shades. For example, the same chemical, fired with abundant air will finish one colour, with no excess air (this is called 'a reducing atmosphere') quite a different one. The manufacturer gives full instructions on the mixing of the pigments but there is usually plenty of scope for experiment, not only in the percentage allowed but also in the combining of different colours. Here it is never safe to assume that the results will necessarily compare with ones experience using water colours or oils. Sometimes the consequence of what began as a straightforward mix may be quite surprising. Always keep a written record of anything you do with pigments, then if, by chance, you obtain a startling and unexpected result you will be able to reproduce it again if you so wish.

Some pigments are intended to be added to powdered clay and then water to form a coloured slip. Others just need water alone. These two are the underglaze stains and may differ slightly from those which are dissolved with glaze powder and are therefore applied after the completion of the biscuit firing. There is a fourth range of colours known as *overglaze enamels* and *lustres*, which are painted on to the finished glazed surface and require an extra firing to make them permanent.

To prepare a slip stain it is usual to work with a white powdered clay which must match exactly the properties of the body to which it is to be applied. This is vital because, if the body expands or contracts at a different rate from the slip attached to it, the coating will peel away and the article will have to be scrapped. Sometimes this tendency does not develop until the final gloss firing at which stage it is most disheartening. By deviating from the recommended percentage of pigment to clay, not only can the shade be made lighter or deeper but, as already hinted, occasionally new and unexpected ones may appear. The slip should be sieved before use, for which a number 80 lawn is the coarsest mesh advisable. When it has been brushed through the wire mesh it should be in the form of a smooth creamy fluid of the chosen colour. Pieces can be dipped in the slip to coat the exterior by pressing them down into it up to the brim with the fingers inside. The pot being so treated must not be too dry or it will crack; if, on the other hand, it is too wet it will quickly

74

fall to bits. The best condition is for the article to be quite firm, that is to say, a little beyond the leather hard stage. The bottom should still be soft enough to take a clear indentation with the finger nail. In this state it is still sufficiently moist for the two clays to bond together. This is true no matter how the slip is applied. The immersion should be over in a second or two, but beware of touching the piece for a few hours afterwards as it will become very soft for a while due to the water it has collected. It is not usual to coat both inside and outside surfaces.

A piece with a handle is particularly vulnerable as it may sag and later collapse. Great care is therefore necessary to keep the immersion time to a minimum.

Slip can also be applied in many other ways; with a paintbrush, for example, or by spraying, or trailing from a polythene container or a syringe. Whichever method is adopted there is one point to watch. When a pot or indeed any shape dries, the thinnest walls (especially those at an edge) are the first to lose moisture. Also water tends to work its way downwards so that, even if the piece were of uniform thickness throughout, the bottom would always be damper than the top. Therefore, it frequently occurs that the lower part of a thrown pot, which usually has a thicker wall, is just right for slipping but the rim is already nearly chalk hard and far too dry. Later, in this case, the slip would flake off from the top but would remain securely keyed to the rest of the body. The remedy is to hold the pot upside down and dip the rim for a distance of, say, an inch or two into a bowl of clean water just for a second, and leave to harden again for five minutes before colouring. This wetting must not be delayed too long or the clay surface may tend to flake off or crumble immediately after immersion. If small raised blisters appear when the slip is subsequently applied this also is a sign that the pot was allowed to get too dry.

A thick slip, especially at the rim, is prone to peel off after firing so try and keep the coating thin on this area. Persistent trouble due to this effect can usually be overcome by keeping a supply of very dilute slip with a high percentage of pigment for painting on such zones.

When a pot has been thrown, it is a good plan to invert it and leave it resting on its rim as soon as this can be done safely without damage. The wetter, thicker parts then feed water downwards

76

to the thinner drier sections. The result is a more uniform average moisture level throughout the whole piece.

Whichever way is used to coat the clay, there are many variations which can be introduced to improve the finished effect. Try painting a tile and then scratching a design with a needle or sharp point to reveal the colour of the body beneath. This is a very old art called *sgraffito* work which originated in Italy during medieval times. There are, sometimes, two coatings, one added on top of the other when the first has dried a little. Then, by gauging the depth of the cut, two shades can be brought into the design.

The opportunity to trail coloured slips on damp clay presents a challenge to the artist whether he is working on a tile, dish or vase. Devices such as those which are used for icing when decorating a cake might be pressed into service but pottery craft suppliers have a selection of suitable containers costing only a shilling or so. Slips, which are not too thick, can be handled quite well through cheap hand spray guns or even scent sprays and very pleasing effects where one or more colour blends into another are easy to achieve. One should, however, remember that powdered clay is not to be breathed. If no extraction fan and filter is available, the work should be done out of doors pointing down wind. A cheap industrial mask is a worth while investment, but certainly no chances should be taken. Paper templates cut from magazines or Christmas cards make excellent silhouettes when stuck on to a moist tile or pot and then removed after spraying. A coarser background pattern is obtained by flicking the bristles of a loaded toothbrush. Flecks of half a dozen different colours make a very gay combination when spattered broadcast over any surface either alone or with a paper shape to build up a picture. A series of motifs can be distributed round a pot spun on a wheel or just turned slowly by someone else whilst the slips are flicked on the outside.

Imitation marble is easy to produce by placing some small pools of slips on a flat surface and then shaking the clay vigorously until they run together. Alternatively, put a series of spots along the top outside edge of a pot and allow these to intermingle as they run down. One may resort to a feather or a very light brush to influence the mixing and so control the marbling as it proceeds. Be careful not to use too much slip on anything but a tile, nor to

77

persist too long with the adjustments, or the body of the pot may become saturated and start to collapse.

Pottery colours, as distinct from coloured slip, are applied with fewer limitations. Here one is working with pigment and water; the body itself is being stained so there are no adhesion problems. Some suppliers recommend that the powders are dissolved in special liquid media which they sell with the colours. Ordinary artist's brushes are used and the condition of the clay body is not at all critical. The only problem is that if it should be a little too wet it may not soak up the pigment quite fast enough to give the desired shade. Pottery colours can be painted without danger on to chalk hard body or on to body which has already been biscuit fired. By spinning the pot on the wheel and holding a charged brush against the surface, simple coloured bands can be quickly and accurately arranged. If working on the unfired clay, patterns can be built into the bands with a sharp scratching tool rather like sgraffito work. Such pots need not be glazed on the outside at all and tend to look even more attractive without glaze, as the bands remain rather more sharply defined and the contrast between colours seems to be more pronounced. The reason for this is that some colours seem to fade in the kiln, especially reds and yellows, and this loss appears to be accentuated when glaze is superimposed. If one is particularly troubled with loss of pigments during the biscuit firing, they can be added afterwards instead. Before dipping such pieces in glaze, give them a low temperature firing heating the kiln to say 700 degs. centigrade so as to 'harden on' the colours and so prevent them from smudging when the liquid glaze is applied.

A little more will be said about glaze decoration in the chapter devoted to the glost firing technique. There is, of course, a wealth of opportunity to create designs in this sphere alone and the variety of the colours available is even more prolific. The pigments can be mixed with either opaque or transparent glazes to obtain the desired effects, and can be dabbed, painted or sprayed on to the pot. Bands of pigmented glaze can be applied as the piece is spun on the wheel or globules allowed to run down and mingle with other colours. Flecked effects can be reproduced from materials supplied by the manufacturer, all of which are very attractive. Those who have artistic abilities have plenty of scope for exercising them when decorating pottery.

The final form of decoration used by the potter is the application of a whole range of special chemicals intended to be employed after glazing. These are known as *lustres* and *on-glaze enamels*. They are usually particularly brilliant but they involve a third firing at a temperature of about 700 degs. centigrade. Gold and silver come within this range since such metals would not remain stable on the ware when being subjected to the much greater heat of the earlier firings. Some have to be mixed with fat oil (a concentration of turpentine) or other media to cause them to adhere to the smooth glassy surface until the piece is put in the kiln. On-glaze enamels sometimes can be pressed into service to reclaim an article which might otherwise have been a reject. If, for instance, it is found that one or other pigment has been lost or greatly reduced in intensity whilst a piece is being fired, then it can be refired with a suitable shade of lustre in place of the colour lost, and the substitution is far from obvious.

We have, therefore, a multitude of ways in which clay can be artistically enhanced. A few possibilities which I have tried myself have been described. Whatever pigment is used it must be subsequently fired in the kiln to make it permanent. However, the finished shade may not be the same as the one originally handled and, since pigments are sometimes a little unpredictable in their behaviour, it is wise to try a small test piece or two and examine the results before going too far with a design. Such a precaution may avoid disappointment when a cherished piece finally comes out of the kiln.

6
BISCUIT FIRING

We now come to the process by which the clay is changed from a soft plastic substance into a hard brittle material which is stable and porous. Once the firing is completed the new properties are permanent. There can be no reversal.

When the pieces to be fired have been allowed to dry, they will have contracted considerably. They may even have lost as much as one-sixth of their original height. They will be rigid, brittle and vulnerable to the slightest knock. In this state they are said to be *chalk dry*. Only in this condition is it safe to commence firing. If a pot is still damp it will almost certainly shatter as soon as heat is applied; this is caused by the formation of steam which expands rapidly and exerts enormous pressure. The minor explosion which results may ruin other ware in the kiln to say nothing of damaging the electric elements. Although it seems absolutely dry to touch, in fact, even chalk dry clay still contains a surprising amount of moisture, as will soon be seen when the temperature of the kiln begins to rise. This is why the heat must always be applied very slowly until all the moisture has been freed. Before loading make sure there are no traces of spilt glaze or the remains of old fused cones on the shelves as these might stick to the pot bottoms. Any found must be chipped away with a stout knife.

Pieces which have been painted with slip can usually be picked up with reasonable safety, provided the hands are clean and free of dust, but any which have had pottery colours applied to the surface should be held at points away from the pigment or from the inside. If a colour is inadvertently smudged the damage can often be repaired; use a razor blade to scratch away the smear and then very carefully fill in again with the paint brush. Where a slipped surface is chipped or otherwise marked the piece will at this stage be too dry to correct with slip, and one can either try and make good straightaway with the nearest available pottery colour or wait until after the biscuit firing and use colour before dipping the piece in glaze. In the second alternative there is a risk of the glaze making the colour run unless the pigment is first hardened on by means of a firing to 700 degs. centigrade.

The art in packing a kiln is the fitting of the maximum quantity of ware into a given space. At the same time it is important to see that every part of every article is, so far as is practicable, raised to the same known temperature. In fact, of course, there are considerable variations in temperature in most kilns, although the designer goes to great lengths in rating and spacing the elements in order to avoid this. Fortunately, most clays and, indeed, most glazes have a fairly wide maturing range so that it is generally possible so to position the ware that the heat applied at any particular point falls within the acceptable limits of the material being fired. Nevertheless, in view of the variants confronting him, it is up to the potter to take as many steps as he can to arrange the articles so that they stand a chance, each and every one, of receiving the same amount of heat. Consider, for example, a pot opposite an electric element with its surface perhaps a $\frac{1}{4}$ of an inch away from the incandescent wire. The clay facing the source of heat must be far hotter than that of a similar pot placed behind it in its shadow. Compare this, moreover, with the inside of the same piece which has an additional insulating wall of clay perhaps three-eighths of an inch thick between it and the element. The difference could be at least 30 degs. centigrade. Thus, if the outside is fired only just to the minimum recommended temperature, the internal parts will be underfired and this may later result in crazing of the glaze.

Many kilns have elements running along the bottom as well as the sides and sometimes in the door and back. Even so, pots on the top shelf can easily be far cooler than those placed lower down in the kiln. If one superimposes on this additional discrepancy the ones we have just examined, it is easy to visualise that within the same firing chamber quite startling variations in temperature can occur. These are some of the reasons why the firing of pottery is almost a craft on its own and one which requires considerable care and experience if first class results are to be obtained every time. As usual, the beginner learns the hard way but this process can be made quicker and less frustrating if each success and more especially each failure is analysed and conditions which operated on that occasion studied with the greatest care.

A record book or card index system is essential and this should be kept up to date. Full details of the charge should be entered before firing and the results added after the ware has been examined. It is even worth making a small sketch showing the positions of the pots and the heights of the shelves, where the cones were placed and how the props were arranged. With experience the amount of data can be gradually reduced but the following details can be regarded as the very minimum:

> Date of Firing.
> Time on low heat, number of elements, how connected.
> Time on full heat. Length of soak (if any).
> Cones used and their positions.
> Number of pots and approx. sizes. Shelf positions.
> Electricity consumed.
> Condition of ware after firing.

The articles should have a serial number scratched or painted on the bottom which will serve to identify each one with the kiln procedure. For instance, a piece might be given the number 1/12167T, meaning that it was the first pot on the top shelf fired on the 12th of January 1967. The appropriate record card could indicate exactly where it was placed on the top shelf. If it was later found to be underfired this could be traced to the fact that the shelf was too good a fit between walls, so tending to isolate the upper part of the chamber, and the pot was in the centre and therefore furthest away from the elements. A similar pot close to the first might prove successful because, perhaps, it was put at the back where it was well away from the door and nearer the heat source rising between the edge of the shelf and the wall of the kiln.

When the pieces are being arranged, it is as well to remember that shelves should be as small as possible, consistent with their usefulness in supporting the ware. This is to avoid splitting the chamber into separate compartments. It is far better to allow the pots to overhang the edges a little and so permit the heat to circulate freely. A twelve inch square internal measurement will do best with a shelf no bigger than ten by ten. If it can be even smaller the firing temperature will be a little more uniform. This
82

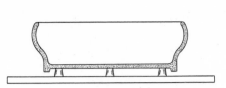

FIG. 52

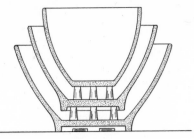

FIG. 53

FIG. 54

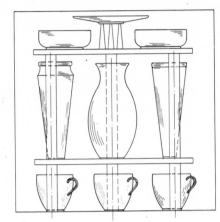

FIG. 55

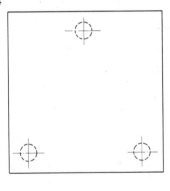

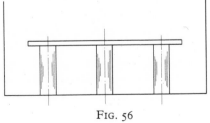

FIG. 56

is why the support in the *Mini-Kiln* is no more than seven by seven in an eight by eight inch chamber.

Although it is true to say that it does no harm if pots touch during the biscuit firing, this is not really to be recommended especially where flat surfaces are concerned. Contact over comparatively large areas tends to isolate the centre of the zone affected and this prevents efficient penetration of the heat. Point contact is acceptable, but even then, where pottery colours have been used, there is a risk of pigment rubbing off or being transferred to places where it is not wanted. Large bowls or dishes will fire better if the bottom is lifted a little off the kiln floor or shelf (figure 52) by resting it on a stilt or on three low props. This also helps to prevent a large flat base bowing downwards and helps to maintain the footring in its correct relative position. The nesting of bowls inside each other, although representing a great economy in space, brings with it the risk of underfiring of those most protected from the heat. Generous spacing with appropriate kiln furniture is the best safeguard (figure 53).

A little forethought during throwing often assists considerably when the time comes to pack the kiln. This is particularly important when space is at a premium as when a small kiln is being loaded. By placing pots with large bases next to those with small ones often the useful charge can be much enhanced (figure 54). Try and fire pieces of approximately the same height in one batch so that the position of the shelf will not be dictated by a single tall article (figure 55). If one is faced with arranging a small number of very large pieces, perhaps, one or two only can be inserted at any one time, have a few small pots ready to fill up the gaps which helps to make the firing less wasteful. It is usually wiser to place a specially bulky and treasured article as close to the centre of the chamber as possible, where it will be heated more evenly and there will be less risk of cracking.

Shelves should always be supported on three props, never four. A fourth has no effect whatever and only monopolises valuable kiln space. They should be set so that, as near as possible, they are positioned at the corners of an imaginary equilateral triangle (figure 56). It is a good plan to put them in their allotted places before loading that layer of pots. Small adjustments to the props can be made where it is obvious that by moving one an inch here

84

or there room can be found for an additional piece. Add the shelf itself last. Leave at least a ¼ of an inch clearance between the top of the tallest pot and the underside of the shelf to allow the heat to reach the inside. The top shelf usually accommodates more ware than the others because there are no props. It may, however, be the one which is coolest of all because often it receives the least direct radiation. Pieces set close to the kiln roof, therefore, may tend to be underfired and it is well worth leaving a little more height than would appear necessary, thus exposing as many side elements as possible to the articles grouped there. Tests with cones left at strategic points, where low heat is suspected, will soon prove whether the variation is serious or not.

At least one *cone* has to be inserted somewhere in the firing chamber, unless the temperature is being measured with a pyrometer, an expensive instrument which usually only takes readings at a fixed point. The cone must, obviously, be visible from the spyhole, so it should be mounted somewhere near the door. However, if it is not too close to the hole it may be affected by draughts, and if too near an element it may give a false indication due to the radiant heat falling on its surface. The best position is a little way from the spyhole, in line with it so that it can be seen surrounded by pots. Sometimes there is very little room for the cone, but with care one can so set it that it will fall neatly between two pots without touching either. Plant its base in a small lump of Pyruma cement so that its ridge leans at an angle of about 15 degs. It should bend along the lower flat side (figure 57), and when the tip is approximately level with the bottom the correct temperature has been reached. One has to be a little cautious in interpreting the behaviour of Seger cones because their temperature of collapse is related to the rate of heat rise. This is assumed by the manufacturer to be about 4 degs. centigrade per minute. Therefore, if the temperature rise is slower the cone will tend to bend at a lower figure than shown on the table, and if the rate is greater than 4 degs. centigrade per minute the cone will tend to fall at a higher temperature. Frequently one sees recommendations that three cones are used. By taking consecutive numbers, warning is given as the critical temperature is approached. Since the rise tends to be quite slow and since there are often so many variations of temperature present within the kiln at the same time, one may be pardoned for questioning whether such elaborate precautions are really necessary in a small unit. Even if it has not fallen, a cone should never be used a second time as its properties may have been affected by its first heating.

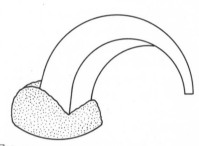

FIG. 57

The standard Seger cone is 2½ inches high. It is manufactured from special materials which soften after a given time at known temperatures. Potters firing earthenware use those numbered from No. 017 to No. 6 corresponding to a temperature range of from 730 degs. centigrade to 1200 degs. centigrade. There are three categories or groups of cones which are most commonly used:

017–015 for lustres and transfers
04–01 for glazes
1–4 for biscuit.

The particular numbers within these three groups which you stock will depend upon the materials you are firing. I mainly use:

No. 017 for lustres
No. 04 for glaze
No. 4 for biscuit.

There is no necessity to stock more than three numbers unless you are going to experiment with other glazes and bodies.

The pundits would probably say that this is an oversimplification, but I have been able to manage quite well on such a restricted arrangement with no apparent trouble. Miniature cones are also available. These stand $1\frac{1}{4}$ inches high and appear to be reliable. They take up much less space and are essential for the *Mini-Kiln*. If there is no convenient shelf at the right height on which to mount the cone so that it can be seen, fit it on a prop. If necessary pack up the prop itself on other furniture until a good view is possible. If the pyruma used to hold the cone is not too wet, it will not stick to the shelf. The cone will, however, fuse to anything it touches as it collapses. Should the cone start bending in the direction of a pot so that in spite of previous precautions it is going to strike the surface, trouble can sometimes be averted as follows. Switch off the electricity. Take a stiff piece of steel rod or fencing wire and very gently pull the tip to one side being careful not to dislodge it from its support and so cause an even worse disaster. Switch on again and try and judge the progress of the cone as it bends to fix the correct temperature to finish the firing.

When all is ready with the cone or cones in position, the door can be closed. The spyhole plug should be left out for a while until all evidence of moisture escaping has disappeared. At first the temperature has to be raised extremely slowly. Instructions for handling the *Mini-Kiln* are given later. Larger electric units, that is to say of one cubic foot or more, usually have at least three elements. It is generally possible, by certain switching arrangements, so to connect these that two are *in series*. This is an electrical term which means that the end of one element is joined to the beginning of the next so as to lower the current passing through both. This drastically reduces the rate of heat release so that the interior of the kiln heats up very slowly indeed. Another method is to fit a *simmerstat* or regulator. This device consists of a little instrument which has a bimetal reed inside it. The reed bends under the influence of a tiny hot element and keeps making and breaking the electrical circuit. The proportion of the *on* period is adjustable by turning a knob. Thus it is possible to choose how quickly the pots will warm up and so control the firing cycle from start to finish. Where the load exceeds 2 kilowatts

87

it would be advisable to combine the simmerstat with a relay or contactor. Full details of all the above wiring arrangements are given in the Appendix.

No attempt should be made to increase the rate of firing until the steam has ceased to issue from the spyhole in quantity. This may take one to two hours. Even then caution is still necessary and the progress towards full load should continue in stages. First set one element run at *full*, followed, say an hour later, by another, and finally the third, when the kiln has been on for about four or five hours. The total biscuit cycle should not take less than eight hours and the slower the temperature rise the better. In the early stages this allows plenty of opportunity for the moisture to escape and later for the heat to penetrate right through to the inside of the clay. When the cone chosen is seen to bend so that its top is level with the base it is time theoretically to turn off the power. However, there are many people, I am one, who advocate a *soak* for at least thirty minutes at about two-thirds of the full load. If the switching arrangements do not permit this to be done, it is worth firing on for ten minutes or so after the fall of the cone to make sure of full heat penetration.

The length of time to allow for the cooling down process will depend upon the kiln: its size, its charge, and the insulating properties of its walls. At least eight to twelve hours should normally elapse until it is safe to open the door. Each piece should then undergo a detailed inspection. If any are cracked, these are best scrapped. But some may be repaired as follows, assuming that the crack is in the bottom where they normally appear; it may go right through, or it may only be on the surface. Take some soft clay and squeeze it very tightly into the affected part, keep it moist until you have smoothed it off level with the rest of the pot, then re-fire it up to normal biscuit temperature after which it should be found that the repair is almost invisible. The piece can then be glazed as usual. Unfortunately a crack in the rim which breaks through to the edge is virtually un-mendable and in this event the pot should be scrapped. A small crack may become much bigger during the glost firing and so, unless the piece has been mended, throw it away and avoid wasting more space and power. Occasionally one finds that little slivers of coloured slip have flaked away from the body. This may have been caused by the slip not fitting the clay of the pot

88

(the powdered clay having different properties), the pot having been too dry when the coating was applied, or the slip being too thick. Frequently this damage can be corrected. Match the shade of the slip with a little pottery colour dissolved in water and carefully paint this on to the affected area. If it still stands out, it may be possible to blend it in to the surrounding part by lightly smudging with the fingertip. Flaking often occurs near the rim where the piece is usually driest when being painted. If during decorating the rim is given a black band or kept to some dark shade it is always easier to hide such a defect, as black or brown pottery colour can then be used. It is wiser to re-fire any biscuit which has been touched up so as to burn in the pigment and prevent it running when the piece is dipped in glaze.

Pots should be protected from moisture and dust until they have been coated with glaze. Fingerprints contain grease which also interferes with the next process, so the less the pieces are handled the better will be the results. If the kiln is still warm, keep the door closed so as to retain as much heat as possible and this will save current if the next firing is to take place almost at once.

7
GLAZING

Fired biscuit ware is usually of little practical value until it has been glazed. This process adds a coating of a glasslike substance and makes the pot watertight. Most glazes are a mixture of three main ingredients. Silica to impart the glassy effect, alumina to blend with the clay body itself and a flux which assists the fusion process and so tends to fix the temperature at which the glaze matures in the kiln. Some glazes, however, are very simple indeed. Common salt, for instance, is frequently used commercially for coating earthenware pipes; however, it would hardly be the choice of the amateur with a small electric kiln. Certain compounds of lead are also used but these introduce a risk to health unless very careful precautions are taken; they should be avoided as there are plenty of equally satisfactory alternatives with no such inherent hazard. It is true that it is possible to combine both biscuit and glaze firings, but it is far safer, and better control can be exerted, if the two operations are performed quite separately. Some potters still mix their own glazes, buying the various chemicals and blending them to obtain special effects. This requires skill and experience, and the majority of potters are satisfied with the prepared commercial product which generally comes in a powdered form only needing to be mixed with water before use. The colouring agents may be acquired independently and added before dissolving, or they may be supplied ready blended in the correct proportions. It will be found that it is easier to dissolve the powder if warm water is used and a rough guide at this stage is to add about $\frac{3}{4}$ of a pint to a pound of dry glaze. This must be sieved, for which a 120 lawn is suitable. The resulting liquid should weight about 30 oz. to the pint.

Powdered glaze frequently is supplied packed in polythene bags or tins in a slightly damp state. This is to prevent scatter of harmful dust, so always try and keep it in this condition.

The glaze liquid is really a suspension of fine particles in water, and the coating process depends upon the fact that biscuit ware is porous. When the fluid comes into contact with the body, the moisture quickly enters the fine pores in its surface but the solids are deposited on the outside forming a thin layer of powder.

The higher the firing temperature of the biscuit the denser is the body likely to be, and therefore the less able to accept water into its pores. Such a pot will need a thicker glaze if an adequate coating is to be deposited on the surface. Experiment will show if the solution is too thin and in this case the weight may have to be increased to as much as 33 oz. to the pint in particular circumstances.

If both outside and inside surfaces are to be coated with glaze, they can both be treated in a single movement. Grip the pot near the base with the fingers and thumb and plunge it rim down quickly into a bucket of the mixture making sure that there is no air cushion inside to prevent the liquid reaching right into the interior. The beginner may find this can be avoided by turning the piece on its side and giving it a rolling motion before withdrawing. The experts have a neat method of their own which can only be acquired with practice. This involves a smart lifting motion and an immediate second immersion, which sends a curtain of fluid licking the inside, whilst the piece is in the inverted position. Assuming that you have been successful in coating most of the pot, there will probably be a few small parts to be covered, for example, where the bottom was held. These are dealt with using a soft paint brush loaded with glaze. It will be easier to do this if the pot is allowed to dry. It may even be slipped into the kiln for five minutes at full heat to evaporate surplus water from the points where it is intended to apply additional glaze. This is sometimes necessary because the whole process depends, as has been described, upon the body soaking up the fluid and leaving the deposit on the outside. If, therefore, the pot is wet, having been already immersed or held too long in the solution, saturation point has been reached and the pot will not soak up moisture. The liquid runs off, and no coating remains on the surface. It is essential therefore to dry the piece thoroughly before making a second attempt. If all has gone well and you have succeeded in obtaining a good covering, any

91

unevenness left at odd points may be very carefully rubbed away with the finger or brush before placing in the kiln. When quite dry a pot can be handled carefully, but never when still even slightly moist. If it is at all damp or the surface tacky, there is a distinct risk of the powder sticking to the fingers and leaving a bald patch. Fortunately, this damage can, of course, be corrected with a brush later.

Jugs, cups and tankards can be conveniently glazed by dipping the piece into the bucket without bothering to immerse the handle at first. Later, when dry, this can be separately dipped or painted with a brush.

When you *dunk* your pot it comes out shiny and wet, but the surface should appear to dry in a minute or so. If it remains obviously wet and the glaze is tending to run down to the bottom there is more than one possible explanation. Firstly, the biscuit may be too dense for the grade of glaze being used, in which case it should be allowed to dry thoroughly and re-done using a thicker solution (even up to 33 oz. to the pint). Secondly, the pot may have been immersed too long, so that the interior of the body has become saturated. Remember that a quick dip is all that is necessary. A second immersion of an already wet pot will do little good and may, on the contrary, cause the loss of some of the powder already deposited. If, therefore, the glaze is tending to run off perhaps in tiny rivulets, dry the pot quickly in the kiln, which may be still warm from the previous biscuit firing. Keep the piece inside until you can hardly bear to hold it in the hand and then, using a brush loaded with thick glaze, repaint the affected parts.

When working with transparent coloured glazes, and if you are aiming for an even coating, some care is necessary. There is a chance that any subsequent correction or adjustment will appear as a blemish due to variations in the thickness of the pigment. Even final handling of the finished dry pot can only be performed with extreme caution. One of the best ways to achieve uniform application is to proceed as follows. Fill a jug with the glaze which is to be used for the inside (which is usually a clear one), fill the pot to the brim and then promptly pour back into the jug or bucket. Any liquid which has slopped down the outside can be wiped away with a damp cloth. If the article has a thick wall it will not be long before the next step can be taken.

92

If it is thin, then the moisture which entered the pores from the inside will have quickly soaked through to the exterior and it would be useless to attempt to apply glaze to the outside until it has dried. If the piece was warm initially the delay will be much less. When quite dry, and after thoroughly stirring the glaze so that the density is the same at the top of the bucket as at the bottom, grip the pot with the fingers from the inside. Use two hands for additional steadiness. Plunge quickly right up to the brim with a steady motion so as not to create ripples, and instantly withdraw. Should the coloured glaze not have quite reached the tidemark of the transparent deposit, it is permissible to extend the clear glaze carefully with a brush when the body is dry again so that there is no gap.

If, in spite of all precautions, the coloured glaze gets smudged or the surface marked in any other way there is nothing to prevent the pot being washed clean under the tap, thoroughly dried and the whole glazing process repeated.

Fired biscuit ware may sometimes be found to be a little denser on the outside than within. This is due to the insulating properties of the body itself by which the temperature of the inner wall, shielded from the direct heat of the kiln, is lower. To deal with this situation, it is convenient to have two glaze solutions prepared. One at 30 oz. to the pint for the inside and another at 32 for the exterior.

Pots which are to be used purely for display or for flowers, plants and so on, are sometimes very attractive if the external glaze coating is omitted, and only the inside is treated, to make the body watertight. The subdued pastel shades which can be obtained by leaving the *matte* finish on the outside are preferred by many to the glossy more commercialised effect of a shiny surface.

Figures are of course only glazed on the visible surface. Any which finds its way on to parts where it is not wanted is quite easily removed by wiping with a damp cloth. In fact, before placing in the kiln, each piece must have its base or footring carefully wiped clean of all traces of powder. If this is not done the article will fuse to the kiln shelf and probably crack later when cooling. There is no need to clean beyond the part actually in contact with the support; provided the glaze is not too thickly applied and the right temperature is used, it should not run during the firing process. The correct thickness is difficult to describe but the following rules may help. The coating should tend to hide the slight inevitable roughness of the fired biscuit. The surface of the powder should therefore appear quite smooth but would still show the ridges which are made by the fingers or turning tool. If the pot is made from red clay, or has any markings or designs, these should just be visible when the piece is first dipped but will be hidden as it dries. If any very narrow ridges of thicker deposit appear, beware, for this may indicate a crack in the body which if verified should perhaps be scrapped. Small irregularities or lumps in the coating are not disastrous and can be ignored as they will spread somewhat as the glaze melts and unless they are very pronounced will hardly show later. If one wishes to be meticulous, they can be rubbed off but one has to do this outside the kiln so as to avoid dropping particles of glaze on to the kiln bottom or shelves.

Many prefer to glaze the footring as well, as this leaves the part of the pot on which it will subsequently rest quite smooth. The circle inside the ring can then be wiped and the pot left standing on a refractory support which will leave the glazed part lifted clear of the shelf. If the whole of the pot is to be coated it has to be supported on what is called a fireclay stilt. This is a star shaped device with sharp points (figure 58). The size should be

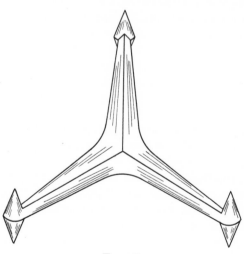

FIG. 58

94

such that the edges are well away from the footring. The glaze will fuse to the three upper points so that the stilt may be firmly attached to the underside when it cools. On the other hand, if there is any degree of differential contraction, it may crack and so become disengaged of its own accord. In any case it will be necessary to chip or grind away the remains of the tips of the stilt after the pot is cool (the end of a file is usually very effective for this purpose). Stilts are cheap and can often be used again by turning them over to leave the other set of points to carry the pot. After that they are normally discarded.

Any grit or dust present in the kiln during the gloss firing is likely to impair the smooth finish. To avoid deposit of such solids, the roof, walls and all shelves, props, etc. should be brushed down before the pots are placed. Even the hole for the spyhole plug should be blown through and the plug itself wiped. Every time it is removed and replaced there is a risk of small particles being carried in suspension and then dropped on to the sticky surface of the melting glaze.

Articles may be placed in the kiln immediately after coating, even if they are quite damp. Obviously they should be so arranged that no two glazed surfaces touch. Neither should they have contact with props or the kiln walls. They can be left quite close to an element without mishap. If any glaze damage is sustained during the placing process, this can be made good by dabbing with a brush at the affected part provided, of course, that the surface is sufficiently dry to absorb the moisture. These last minute final touches may seem very rough and ugly but with clear glaze this is not important.

When all the ware is safely stacked, place the cones where they can be observed from the spyhole as with biscuit firing. Set them out so that as they fall, they will not touch any glazed surface. If there is doubt about whether an article will foul the door when it is closed, put a straight edge made from a lath or any convenient material across the opening and this will show the clearance (a stretched piece of string would do). Close the door gently to prevent scatter of grit, take out the spyhole plug and switch to full heat. For the first half hour or so there will be a fair quantity of steam released and it should be allowed to escape freely. This is the water which soaked into the porous biscuit when the glaze coating was being applied. As soon as the

95

steam has disappeared, insert the plug and let the kiln temperature build up to the recommended level. This varies according to the type of glaze being used but is not likely to be below 900 degs. centigrade. One must be guided entirely by the instructions of the supplier and normally there is a reasonably wide range within which the glaze can be matured. If a cone representing the mean figure is chosen, then, once it has fallen, it is wise to continue firing for, say, a quarter of an hour at about two-thirds rate if possible to administer a *soak* which will ensure that all surfaces do indeed reach the required temperature. If the kiln has only one element and therefore only one rate of firing, unless one is prepared to add a simmerstat or exert hand control, it may be possible to extend the heating period at full output as a precaution against underfiring. Ten minutes or even a quarter of an hour at maximum rate would then be worth trying. Experiments made with additional cones will soon show whether the glaze maximum temperature would be exceeded thereby or not. On the whole with ordinary transparent glazes it is better to overfire than to risk underfiring which may result in crazing. This is an effect frequently seen on old tiles where one finds a network of minute cracks in the glossy surface. Overfiring may produce blisters. There is much to be learned through studying the performance of your own kiln and the materials with which you are working. By recording and analysing the results obtained by methodical trial and error, much more can be gained than from any guidance which can be given even in the most detailed manual.

Having reached the correct temperature range and finally turned off the power, one must now, at all costs, resist the temptation to open the kiln too soon. Experienced potters have issued warnings against draughts even from the spyhole which it is said will result in dire consequences. Nevertheless, one may find that no harm is done to the ware by a peep through the hole with a torch a few hours after firing has ceased. Only a potter knows how exciting it is to get the first glimpse of the finished colours in this way. To be absolutely safe, one should not open the kiln until the contents are cool enough to be handled. There are many, however, who regularly don asbestos gloves and remove the pieces when they are still very hot indeed, and they seem to get away with it; I do. This sort of behaviour is probably reasonably safe with simple symmetrical shapes, but if there are figures or pots with handles, beware. Many a cherished work of art has suddenly shattered when cooling due to uneven contraction so it is better to wait if you can. A good plan is to release the door and leave it say one inch open for about two hours when the pots are still too hot to hold and this will speed up the cooling process and allow the emptying of the kiln somewhat earlier than would otherwise be possible. With the *Mini-Kiln*, the top slab could be lifted and wedged open the same amount at one side. Sudden cooling, as well as causing major fractures, can sometimes result in crazing.

Try re-firing pots which have crazed. Then, provided the glaze suits the biscuit on which it is spread, the trouble may disappear. Crazing which results from glost underfiring or too rapid cooling seems to develop quickly. Sometimes, however, pieces may start to craze weeks or even months after being in the kiln. The process starts at one point and extends progressively across large areas of the surface. One can often clearly hear the sharp 'pings' as the tiny cracks spread from one part to another. If this happens, examine the pot carefully and, if you notice that the trouble is spreading from zones which are likely to have been coolest during the biscuit firing, you have a valuable clue. For example crazing which commenced at the bottom inside would be due to underfiring of the biscuit because this is likely to have been the coolest part of the piece. Again, by referring to your kiln records, you may be able to trace where that particular pot was placed during the first firing. If it was on a top shelf, perhaps very close to the roof, this would tend to insulate the interior. It is true to say that the denser the body the less prone is the piece to long term crazing. There is a very good test which you may have seen carried out by experienced potters. After the first firing, check the base of each piece of ware with the tongue. If it sticks to the pot, it is porous; if it comes away without sticking you may be sure that you have a good dense body and, provided the glaze 'fits' the clay, you should not have any trouble in the future from that piece.

Pots which have been raised to too high a temperature during the glost firing may tend to develop blisters, and should go back in the kiln. Before replacing them, however, break the thin skin covering the blister and fill the crater with a little powdered glaze.

97

After re-firing it is possible that the blemish will then be almost completely removed. If, by some misfortune, two pieces have been in contact, they will be fused together and must somehow be separated. This may be disastrous. The best that can happen is that there will be a scar left on the surface of each. If possible grind this down with an old file, press glaze powder into any hole left and re-fire. The damage may not be too obvious.

If it is found that some parts of an article are only thinly covered with glaze so that the rough biscuit can be felt through it, then brush more on to the affected sections and replace in the kiln for the next convenient glost firing. The fresh glaze may be easier to apply if the pot is heated first to about 150 degs. fahrenheit and a thicker than usual mixture is used. Clear glaze will be found to blend perfectly with the original but if one is using colours it may be very difficult, if not impossible, to disguise the adjustment.

Glaze which, after firing, has been found to have run towards the footring or to have smudged the colours on the biscuit underneath, has either been too thickly applied or has been raised to too high a temperature. I know of no remedy for pieces so affected.

Mention has already been made of coloured glazes. There is a very wide choice of stains and these should, at first, be mixed with the glaze powder in the proportions suggested by the supplier. Subsequent experiment is interesting and sometimes very rewarding but it is safer, to begin with, to conform to the known formulae. Transparent coloured glazes are usually applied to white, ivory or buff bodies. If they are put on a red or brown biscuit they will tend to be dominated by the body colour and will become almost invisible. For such a case one would normally use an opaque glaze which completely obscures the body underneath and fires white on its own, or will assume any of the shades which come from the stains mixed with it. Most suppliers stock this material which is prepared in a similar way to ordinary glaze.

There is, of course, no obligation to aim for a perfectly even coating of glaze and there are many artistic effects which deliberately set out to exploit the very opposite. For example, one may apply either a transparent or opaque white glaze by dipping in the usual way and then add others (which are coloured) by brushing, spraying or spattering from the bristles of a stiff brush. Any unevenness tends to be lost in the subsequent firing. Great

98

care in handling is now necessary and it is best to grip all the pieces from the inside, if possible, as the slightest contact will smudge the colours.

It is as well to remember that some glazes may contain salts of lead or other substances more or less harmful and every care is needed to avoid any risk of contaminating household utensils. The hands should always be washed after working with glazes.

For consistent results the following rules must be observed:

Check the weight of powdered glaze per pint of water and combat evaporation by adding more water if necessary.

Always stir glaze thoroughly before and during use and be sure to mix in the sediment at the bottom before attempting to apply it to a pot. Glaze settles quickly and must be kept continually on the move.

Reserve heavier concentrations for denser pots. If two separate supplies are not kept, pour off some of the clear liquid from the top of the bucket and put this on one side whilst treating these articles in the stronger mixture. Later replace the excess liquid and mix again for coating the more porous articles.

Very occasionally it may be necessary to re-sieve. The warning sign is when coarse particles begin to appear, when there is evidence that grit or dust have entered the solution or when nodules are left on an otherwise smooth surface after dipping.

Handle pots as little as possible in the biscuit stage prior to the addition of glaze. Any grease or dust will interfere with the adhesion of the glaze powder and leave blemishes or pinholes which may require correction and re-firing.

Be scrupulously alert against mixing colours by interchange of strainers, jugs, brushes, etc.

Glaze does not deteriorate and can be kept for a prolonged period. Even if allowed to go hard, it can be re-dissolved, sieved and used again.

8
A DESIGN FOR A MINI-WHEEL

Foot operated treadle or kick wheels have tended to be cheaper than those driven by electricity. Moreover many dedicated people feel that only by directly controlling the operation of the wheel can the ultimate perfection be achieved. Personally, I prefer a wheel which is driven mechanically so that I can concentrate entirely upon the clay itself. I am sure that most beginners would be inclined to agree with me. Unfortunately, hitherto, power wheels have generally been rather expensive. Sometimes they have been twice the cost of one worked by foot. This seems to be because the makers have tried to cater simultaneously, in one machine, for two classes of worker. First, for the student who will learn by starting with half a pound or a pound of clay. Second, for the serious studio potter who will perhaps be throwing pieces weighing a couple of pounds for most of the time but has to have the capacity to create a really large specimen now and again. Therefore, those wheels which have been available up to now are usually powerful enough to take at least four pounds of clay and frequently six or ten. This is much more than even the advanced amateur really needs and few, anyway, have a kiln large enough to fire economically such heavy work, even if it can be accommodated at all.

To me it seems absurd to present someone who is only a beginner with anything heavier to throw than one pound of clay. In fact I would tend to commence with even less. This is because the problem of controlling and centering increases rapidly as the size of the lump becomes heavier. Long, tedious attempts to master a big piece only lead to frustration, disappointment, and material which soon becomes too wet to manage anyway. In my opinion, a smaller wheel and less powerful motor is quite sufficient for most students and for many serious workers too.

The two models I am about to describe are rated at 1 lb. and 2 lb. of clay respectively according to the type of motor fitted.

With practice both limits can be greatly exceeded. The first is driven by a special constant speed motor of the shaded pole design. The second by a motor with a commutator. This develops more torque and is, moreover, suitable for working with a resistance so that the speed can be varied. It is very convenient to do this by means of a foot operated pedal which is supplied complete with the kit. Nevertheless, even if you decide on the cheaper single speed design, there is still tremendous scope for the creation of every conceivable shape. The recommended rate for the wheelhead itself with this model is about 120 revolutions per minute, which will permit a pot diameter of fully six inches. The height which can be attained will, of course, depend upon your skill and experience but seven or eight inches is by no means impossible.

I have always contended that the same sort of expertise can be developed on a small scale as can be achieved on much larger machines. The freedom to form beautiful shapes is there whether the clay weighs four ounces or four pounds. I have myself thrown hundreds of miniature pieces, using no more than two ounces of clay, and found these quite fascinating to make.

Whilst the constant speed Mini-wheel is a serviceable appliance, in many ways ideal for the beginner since there is one less factor about which to worry—the speed—it does have limitations. There is a great advantage in being able to alter the R.P.M. whilst throwing is actually in progress. I would, therefore, recommend the more expensive design (especially since there is only a few pounds difference in the cost of the parts) for the more serious amateur potter. The Appendix gives a list of suppliers who will be only too glad to assist in providing the necessary components.

The wheel, completely assembled, is shown in the photograph in Chapter 4. Both models look virtually the same from the outside and have similar overall dimensions. The variable speed foot control unit is simply connected by a flex to the more powerful machine. Either Mini-wheel is easy to carry as it weighs only about 20 lb., and so it can be put away safely in a cupboard when not in use. The wooden casing helps to reduce the weight and it is very simple to assemble, needing no special carpentry experience. The bowl is made of polythene.

The making of the bearing assemblies (figures 59 and 60) are rather outside the province of the ordinary potter unless he has access to a lathe and is a skilled engineer. Arrangements have, therefore, been made for kits of such parts to be obtainable from

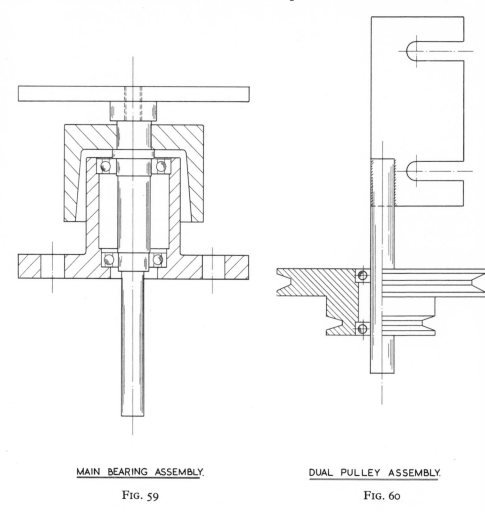

MAIN BEARING ASSEMBLY.

FIG. 59

DUAL PULLEY ASSEMBLY.

FIG. 60

an equipment manufacturer. These are obtainable either as a complete set or separately at quite modest cost. Working drawings can also be procured from the same source should you prefer to machine the components yourself.

If you can make use of a motor already in your possession, this will greatly assist in keeping down expense. It will, however, probably mean that you will have to adjust some of the dimensions of the wooden casing and possibly the lengths of the belts to accommodate it. The speed of the shaded pole motor sold with the cheaper kit is 2500 R.P.M. and its rating is 1/25 horsepower. The commutator motor, the more sophisticated alternative, has a top speed of about 5000 R.P.M. and a rating of roughly 1/12 horsepower. The pulley ratios shown in the list of parts are intended to accommodate both types of drive.

List of parts for the two designs of Mini-Wheel

Motor (either shaded pole of special design or commutator type).

Head assembly complete with spinner and 5-inch wheelhead.

11-inch single groove pulley.

Dual pulley assembly.

Motor pulley.

Polythene bowl—12-inch diameter, $4\frac{1}{2}$ or $4\frac{3}{4}$ inches high.

One set of wooden parts as shown in figure 61.

Four rubber buffers for feet with suitable wood screws.

Three $\frac{3}{8}$ of an inch rubber washers.

One 5-inch diameter rubber disc $\frac{1}{8}$ of an inch thick.

One threeway terminal block with screws for attaching to casing.

One rubber flex sleeve (as used with some electric irons).

Three yards of triple 5-amp cable (only required for constant speed model).

18 inches of copper bare earth wire.

One Fenner endless belt No. 2390. (This may alter with your own motor.)

One $\frac{1}{4}$-inch Singer belt, endless 16 inches long. (Check your motor before buying.)

One pressure operated switch for constant speed motor, OR, one speed control foot unit with flex for variable speed motor.

Two $\frac{5}{16}$ of an inch by $1\frac{1}{4}$-inch bolts (these may be obtainable from your local garage).

Five $\frac{5}{16}$ of an inch washers.

Four $\frac{3}{8}$ of an inch by $1\frac{3}{4}$-inch bolts.

Nine $\frac{3}{8}$ of an inch washers.

Two $\frac{3}{16}$ of an inch by $1\frac{3}{4}$-inch bolts with five washers for fixing motor (these may vary with the motor).

Approximately two dozen 1 inch No. 6 countersunk steel wood screws.

One dozen $\frac{1}{2}$-inch No. 6 countersunk steel wood screws.

An ounce or so of waterproof plastic compound (available at do-it-yourself shops).

One pound of waterproof paint.

Cut out the plywood in accordance with the dimensions shown in figure 61. The exploded view, figure 62, indicates how the pieces should be assembled. 1 inch No. 6 woodscrews are amply strong enough and even $\frac{3}{4}$-inch ones will suffice if necessary. It would do no harm to use one of the modern waterproof adhesives as an additional precaution. Mark off for the four $\frac{3}{8}$-inch bolts for the main head bearing flange and drill $\frac{1}{2}$-inch holes for them. The hole for the shaft is 1 inch in diameter.

The polythene bowl should be about 12 inches in diameter and not more than 5 inches high, either an oval or square bowl would be acceptable provided it was no deeper than this. If too shallow, the water will splash over the edge when the wheel is rotating. If the bowl is wider than 12 inches you can still manage with it, as the head does not necessarily have to be in the centre. It can be off-set so long as the middle hole is $6\frac{1}{2}$ inches from the shelf face as seen in figure 63. One hole an inch in diameter should now be cut for the shaft and the main bearing flange used to mark off for the other four in the bowl. These should be about $\frac{1}{2}$ an inch in diameter. The 5-inch diameter rubber disc is placed between the bearing flange and the bowl. Three of the bolts securing this flange have rubber washers as shown in figure 64A, the fourth has none (figure 64B). This bolt should be nearest to the shelf and will be connected to the earth wire. The omission of the rubber ensures a good electrical contact. To prevent water seeping down to the inside of the casing, squeeze a little of one of the plastic sealing components into the holes before assembling. Tighten up the four bolts only lightly at first to permit a little extra adjustment when you come to fit the belts. Place the large aluminium pulley on the shaft and arrange it with its boss

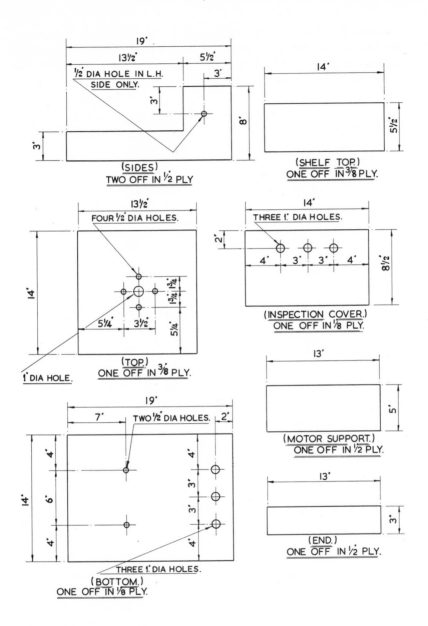

19'

13½'   5½'

½' DIA HOLE IN L.H.
SIDE ONLY.   3'

3'

3'   8'

3'

(SIDES)
TWO OFF IN ½ PLY

14'

5½'

(SHELF TOP.)
ONE OFF IN ⅜ PLY.

13½'

FOUR ½' DIA HOLES.

14'

14'

1¾' 1¾'

5¼'   3½'   5¼'

1' DIA HOLE.

(TOP.)
ONE OFF IN ⅜ PLY.

14'

THREE 1' DIA HOLES.

2'

4'   3'   3'   4'

8½'

(INSPECTION COVER.)
ONE OFF IN ⅛ PLY.

13'

5'

(MOTOR SUPPORT.)
ONE OFF IN ½ PLY.

19'

7'   TWO ½' DIA HOLES.   2'

4'   4'

14'   6'   3'   3'

3'

4'   4'

THREE 1' DIA HOLES.
(BOTTOM.)
ONE OFF IN ⅛ PLY.

13'

3'

(END.)
ONE OFF IN ½ PLY.

FIG. 61

105

downwards, that is to say furthest from the bowl, so as to leave the two Allen fixing screws accessible. The edge of the boss should be about $\frac{1}{2}$ an inch from the end of the spindle. Nip up the screws so as just to locate in position.

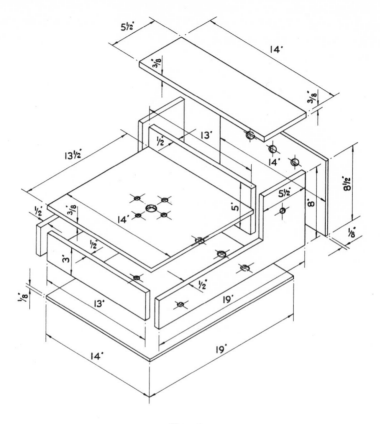

FIG. 62

It is now best to work with the whole casing upside down and the weight taken on the polythene. Run the heavier belt round the large wheel and the smaller diameter groove of the dual pulley. Offer the bracket up to the inside wall of the shelf and mark for the two $\frac{5}{16}$-inch bolts which will secure it to the $\frac{1}{2}$-inch motor support panel. Leave room for later adjustment. Drill two $\frac{3}{8}$ of an inch holes and bolt into position. Make certain that
106

the belt is exactly in line with the grooves so that it will lead smoothly from one to the other. Washers should be used behind both bolt heads and nuts. Check that you are going to have room to mount your motor before going too far at this stage. The motor is secured to the same panel and two $\frac{3}{16}$-inch bolts are quite strong enough for either design. The light belt is taken from the pulley on the motor to the larger of the grooves on the dual

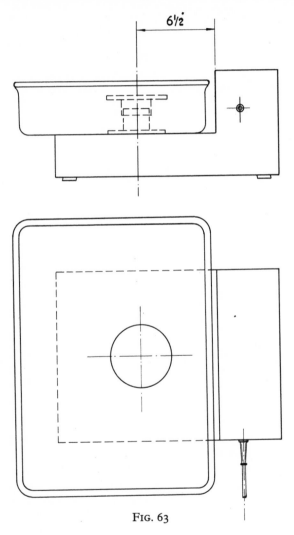

FIG. 63

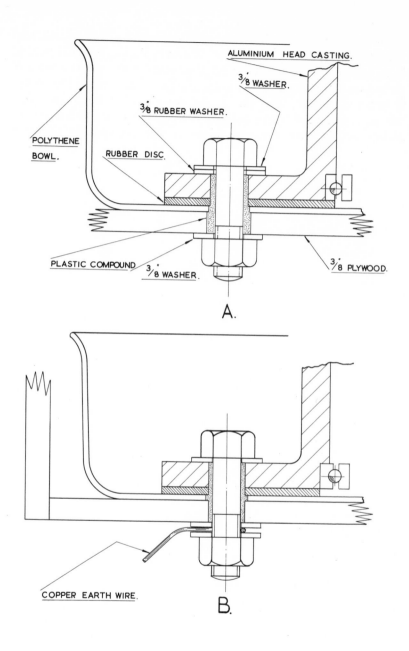

ALUMINIUM HEAD CASTING.

$\frac{3}{8}''$ WASHER.

$\frac{3}{8}''$ RUBBER WASHER.

POLYTHENE BOWL.

RUBBER DISC.

PLASTIC COMPOUND.

$\frac{3}{8}''$ WASHER.

$\frac{3}{8}''$ PLYWOOD.

A.

COPPER EARTH WIRE.

B.

FIG. 64A and B

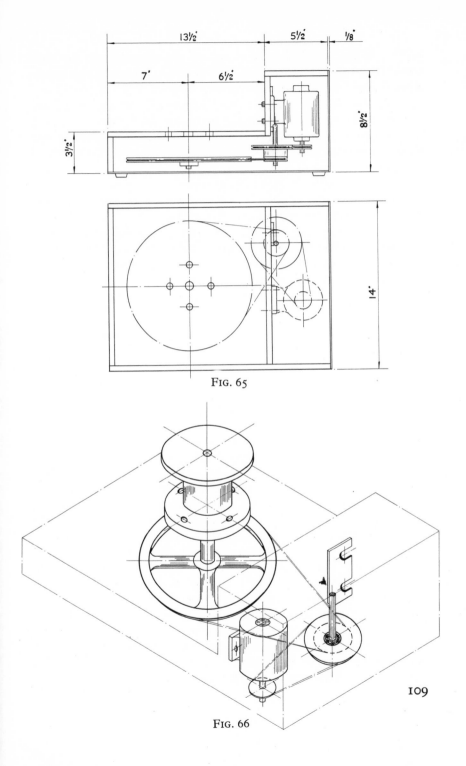

FIG. 65

FIG. 66

109

pulley. When looking on the end of the motor shaft, rotation should be in a clockwise direction. Therefore, when the machine is turned over into the normal working position the wheelhead will rotate anti-clockwise. This is very important. When setting the motor in place, once more make provision for future tensioning of the drives. After you are satisfied with the alignment and tightness of the two belts it is time to secure everything firmly in position.

Fit a threeway terminal strip at some convenient point on the inner wall and drill a $\frac{1}{2}$-inch hole in the nearest side for the rubber sleeve. Thread the triple-core flex through the sleeve leaving plenty of spare cable and pull the rubber and the wire so as to lock firmly in the hole. To be on the safe side it is wise to clamp the flex with a piece of wood cut with a V groove to prevent it ever being drawn out of the casing (figure 67).

The colour coding convention for electrical cables is about to be changed, so the old and the new systems are given below.

PRESENT BRITISH STANDARD		FUTURE STANDARD
Live wire	Red	Brown
Neutral wire	Black	Blue
Earth wire	Green	Green with yellow bands

Lock each of the three coloured leads in a socket in the threeway terminal block as shown in figure 67. Remember that the green one or the green one with yellow bands is the earth and this is used as a protection in case there is ever an electrical leakage from the live terminal. Should this occur, then the electricity will flow back to earth blowing a fuse before it can do any harm or administer a dangerous shock. Therefore take great care to ensure that any metal part is connected to this wire. The following instructions should be faithfully observed in the interests of safety. Run a length of bare wire from the socket with the earth to the nearest $\frac{3}{8}$ of an inch bolt holding down the main bearing assembly, trapping it beneath the extra washer as shown in figure 64B. Clean the two washers first to free them from all traces of dirt or rust. Do the same inside the casing with one of the $\frac{5}{16}$-inch bolts at the dual pulley bracket. If the motor has only two wires issuing from it, then its chassis must also be connected to earth. This can be done by releasing one of the nuts or screws holding it together and inserting the wire behind it before re-tightening.

110

Once again scrape the parts clean of paint or anything which would prevent a good metallic contact being made. If the motor already has a third wire coming from the inside this may be green or green with yellow bands, in which case its frame is

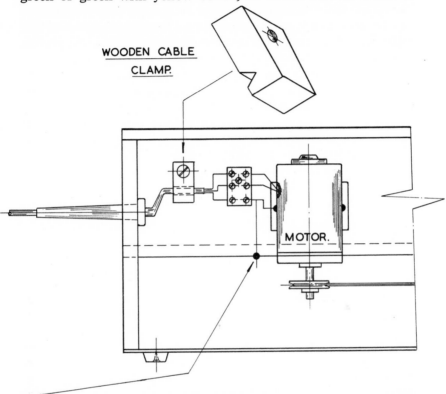

WOODEN CABLE
CLAMP.

MOTOR.

EARTH WIRES LEAD TO MOTOR FRAME, TO DUAL PULLEY BRACKET AND TO NEAREST $\frac{3}{8}$" BOLT OF MAIN BEARING ASSEMBLY.

FIG. 67

coupled to it internally. It is then only necessary to lead this one direct to the earthing socket in the block.

The foregoing precautions are very important indeed. As a final safeguard you should have your work checked by a qualified electrician before you connect your wheel to the supply.

The other two leads feed the motor and are simply taken to the windings via the remaining sockets in the triple block.

111

Obviously the motor has to be stopped and started so a switch is required somewhere in the electrical circuit. This has to be arranged to break the live wire. That is to say, it must interrupt the supply at the red or brown lead. When throwing is in progress the hands are wet so it is not safe to do this with an ordinary switch as these are not usually easily obtainable in a waterproof form. It is much better to control the wheel with a foot switch. This can always be kept dry and at the same time it leaves the

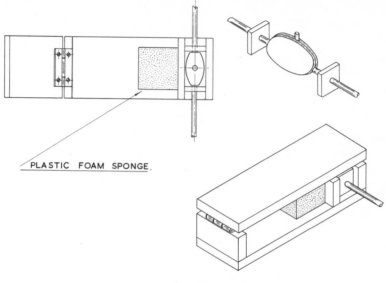

PLASTIC FOAM SPONGE.

FIG. 68

hands free which is a great advantage. The design shown in figure 68 is suggested for the constant speed wheel. This is quite easy to assemble from pieces of wood obtainable in any do-it-yourself shop and the switching device itself is part of the kit. The block of plastic foam sponge acts like a spring to lift the hinged pedal when the pressure of the foot is released. The switch of course does not have to break the neutral wire; only the live one.

The variable speed motor is available complete with its foot controller fully wired ready for connecting to the leads from the wheel at one side and to the mains plug at the other. Nevertheless whichever design you are assembling be sure to take no risks and have a thorough check made before you think of trying your handiwork on 230 volts.

Squeeze a little soft bearing grease into the two ball races in the dual pulley and wipe away all surplus to avoid the lubricant being thrown outwards on to the belts when the machine is running. Put some more on the exposed race at the top of the main bearing assembly. Now drop the aluminium spinner on to its shoulder on the shaft and screw the head disc in position. Attach the bottom panel with ½-inch wood screws and add the four rubber buffers at the corners. These will raise the casing about ½ an inch off the table and allow air to circulate through the cooling holes. Last of all fit the inspection panel. This also can be held in place by ½-inch screws. Never connect to the electric supply until this panel is there to protect you from the live wires and moving parts.

To throw with the Mini-wheel, place it on a firm table so that the bowl is furthest from you. You can then rest your forearms on the raised shelf which houses the motor. This you will find is the most convenient position. Protect the top of your table if you are worried about it getting wet or spotted with grease. Place the controller on the floor so that you can press on it with your foot. It will be more comfortable if you rest your heel on a thick book or a block of wood and just use the toe to actuate the switch or speed regulator.

The aluminium wheelhead should have the slightest trace of moisture on its surface. When you fling the lump of clay on to it, work it gently towards the centre until it runs reasonably true. This will reduce the mechanical load on the motor when you come to commence the first operation. The initial centering will take a little longer with the single speed model.

Here are a few special points to watch when you are using your Mini-Wheel.

Always be sure to have the spinner in place as this protects the ball races in the main bearing and prevents water or clay reaching them. Never allow the water in the bowl to rise above the flange of the aluminium housing. That is to say it should not be more than ½ an inch deep. After using the wheel, reclaim any odd bits of clay or slurry for the scrap bucket and empty the water into the sink or elsewhere to waste. Be sure to disconnect from the supply first, by switching off at the mains and withdrawing the

113

plug from the house socket. Never carry the Mini-Wheel whilst it is switched on. If you wish, you may find it easier to mop up the surplus water with a cloth which can then be wrung out until all is removed. Try and keep the wooden casing dry and always prevent water reaching the wires or the internal electrical parts.

After throwing is finished, thoroughly dry all the machine. Take off the wheelhead disc and the spinner. Wipe them clean and put a few drops of oil on the thread. The disc is removed by unscrewing anti-clockwise looking at it from above. If it is too tight to release, proceed as follows: Disconnect from the supply, turn the whole machine on its side, insert a screwdriver or poker through one of the $\frac{1}{2}$-inch holes in the bottom panel so that it passes between the spokes of the big pulley. Now grip the disc and twist anti-clockwise and it should disengage satisfactorily.

Occasionally check the belt tension; one which slips will quickly wear out, and a belt which is too tight may overload the motor. Never make any adjustment with power still connected to the machine. Always unplug it from the mains first. The cooling holes in the casing are necessary to permit air to circulate over the motor, so make sure that they are never obstructed. If, when throwing, you stall the motor, relax your grip on the clay immediately so as to allow it to restart. If you hold it locked with the current on you may damage the windings. If the motor fails to start, try first turning the wheelhead. If this does not get it going, disconnect from the supply and search for the cause. There may be something jammed in the drive. However, if the fault is electrical you should call for expert assistance.

Provided the foregoing precautions are observed and a little grease applied to the top race of the main bearing occasionally, the Mini-Wheel should run for many hours with no further attention. With it you will be able to create almost anything which can be made on much larger and more expensive equipment.

9
BUILDING YOUR MINI-KILN

There is nothing at all difficult about assembling a small pottery kiln and it will fire efficiently provided certain basic principles have been properly observed. Firstly, the interior has to be constructed from material which will withstand the very high temperatures which are necessary to change the clay into pot. Secondly, the walls have to have good insulating properties so as to retain the heat released in the interior. Thirdly, the rate of heat generation must exceed the rate of loss through radiation throughout the temperature range within which the kiln is to operate. Whilst wood or gas firing are frequently used as alternative sources of fuel, there is no doubt that electricity is by far the most convenient for the amateur. The unit about to be described can be plugged into the ordinary house mains. It can, moreover, be built with practically no previous engineering or bricklaying experience. The work is really so simple that it can easily be completed within the space of a weekend using tools which would be normally readily available. Arrangements have been made for kits of parts to be obtainable from a specialist supplier but, in case you prefer to buy these piecemeal, a complete list of all the materials used is given below.

List of parts required to build Mini-Kiln

Asbestos

1 asbestos base board $17'' \times 13\frac{7}{8}'' \times \frac{1}{2}''$	To place under kiln.
2 asbestos sheets $14'' \times 13\frac{1}{2}'' \times \frac{1}{4}''$	For side with spyhole.
2 asbestos sheets $14'' \times 14'' \times \frac{1}{4}''$	For opposite long side.
4 asbestos sheets $12'' \times 14'' \times \frac{1}{4}''$	For ends of kiln.
1 asbestos sheet $11\frac{3}{4}'' \times 13\frac{3}{4}'' \times \frac{1}{4}''$	For fitting below bottom slab.
18'' of stranded asbestos rope	Used for sealing joints.
8 $1'' \times 1'' \times \frac{1}{2}''$ pads	Spacers for below kiln.

Insulating Material (H.T.1 quality)

4 slabs $12'' \times 7'' \times 4''$	For base and cover of kiln.
4 bricks $12'' \times 4\frac{1}{2}'' \times 2''$	For long walls.
4 bricks $10'' \times 4\frac{1}{2}'' \times 2''$	For short walls.

Steel Parts

4 steel angles 14″ × 1½″ × 1½″ × ¼″	For corners of kiln body.
4 steel angles 3½″ × 1½″ × 1½″ × ⅛″	For corners of cover.
4 Jubilee clips 5″ diameter	For clamping together.
4 Jubilee clips 4½″ diameter	For clamping together.
1 ³⁄₁₆-twist drill or piercing tool	For making holes in base.
1 ⅛″-twist drill or piercing tool	For making holes to fix elements.

Electrical Parts

2 Kanthal elements in No. 20 S.W.G. wire	For winding on tiles.
48″ 5-amp asbestos covered cable	For connecting up elements.
4 5-amp porcelain single way connectors	For connecting elements to asbestos cables.
1 10-amp threeway terminal strip	For connecting mains to asbestos cables.
1 steel conduit box with lid	To house electrical parts.
18″ bare copper earth wire	To earth kiln.
1 earthing clamp with screw nut and washer	For attaching earth wire to one Jubilee clip.
48″ No. 20 S.W.G. Kanthal wire	For attaching tiles to end walls of kiln.
1 rubber sleeve	For leading in mains cable.
2 screwed bushes with nuts	For protecting sharp edges at holes in conduit box.
3 yards triple core 10-amp mains flex	For feeding kiln.

Sundries

2 refractory element tiles (special)	For holding Kanthal wires.
8 1″-wire nails	For attaching pads to board.
1 No. 6 woodscrew 1″ long	For fixing threeway strip.
2 No. 6 woodscrews ½″ long	For attaching conduit box to asbestos base.
1 ½″-4.B.A. setscrew and washer	For connecting earth wire to conduit box.
1 pound Pyruma cement (or equivalent)	For making spyhole plugs and sundry uses.
1 kiln shelf 7″ × 7″ × ½″	For use when firing kiln.
9 props approx. 1½″ high	For supporting shelf.
A supply of suitable pyrometric cones	For estimating temperature.

The kiln must rest on a firm foundation of brick or concrete. Failing all else, it can be placed on a domestic hearth providing there is nothing inflammable near it. The bottom asbestos sheet, as well as the sides, will get very hot indeed, so beware, as there could be a risk of cracking tiles, though I think this is rather unlikely. The kiln should never be left outside where it might become damp, as at all times it must be kept absolutely dry.

Before commencing the assembly, there is some preparatory work to be done. Drill two $\frac{3}{16}$ of an inch holes in each of the refractory base blocks in the positions shown in figure 69. The same illustration indicates the four matching holes of the same diameter which are required in the $11\frac{1}{4}$ inch by $13\frac{3}{4}$ inch asbestos sheet on which the pair of blocks are supported. They are used to take the leads from the electric elements which will eventually supply the heat for firing the kiln. It will be found that both types of material are quite soft and so easy to cut. An ordinary twist drill will pass through without any difficulty. The standard length, however, may prove a little short and, as it is not too easy to drill the slabs from opposite sides, the following suggestion may be useful. Obtain a 6 inch length of $\frac{3}{16}$ of an inch round bar or, better still, silver steel from your nearest blacksmith or stockist. Now file three flats at the end so as to give it a diamond point. When used in an ordinary hand brace this *bit* will easily cope with either the insulating brick or the asbestos. Use only moderate pressure especially when about to break through at the far side so as to avoid damage to the material as the point emerges.

One of the 12 inch long bricks has to have a spyhole cut in it as explained in figure 70. If you can get a $\frac{3}{4}$-inch augur, as used for wood, this will be quite satisfactory but do not be surprised if it needs sharpening afterwards! You can, of course, manage with the $\frac{3}{16}$ of an inch piercing tool and open out the hole to the required diameter or something approaching it with a penknife. The exact size is not very important.

Lay the brick so prepared on one side, it will be needed later.

Now take the $\frac{1}{2}$ inch thick asbestos base and cut two slots in it with a hacksaw, as indicated in figure 71. Make eight $\frac{1}{2}$ inch $\times$ 1 inch $\times$ 1 inch asbestos pads and nail these firmly in place, spacing them approximately as suggested in the drawing. These are needed to maintain a gap below the kiln and so leave room for the wires which feed the elements.

There are still two 1 inch diameter holes to make in the 14 inch $\times$ $13\frac{1}{2}$ inch asbestos front sheets, and 2 inch $\times \frac{1}{4}$ inch slots in the bottom for the cables. See figure 72. This illustration also explains how the various pieces will eventually be assembled.

Now mount the two bottom slabs with the holes on their asbestos sheet and place in position on the spacing pads. The

118

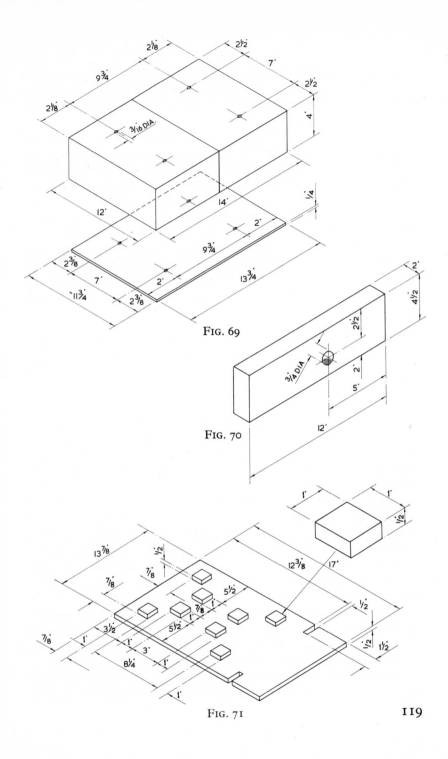

FIG. 69

FIG. 70

FIG. 71

long face of the combined block so formed should be level with the shorter edge of the $\frac{1}{2}$ inch thick base as shown in figure 73. The thin asbestos sheet will, of course, come about $\frac{1}{8}$ inch from the block on all sides.

Shred the asbestos rope so as to obtain about two dozen separate strands. These will be used to assist in reducing air leaks between the parts of the kiln lining. Lay two rows of the string you have just prepared round the base blocks and bed the first 10 inch long brick on these as is shown in figure 74. It rests on one of its 2 inch sides with the $4\frac{1}{2}$ inch face vertical and in line with the wall of the base block. Prepare the end of one of the 12 inch bricks with a loop of asbestos string as in figure 75A. It is not difficult to make the fibrous material adhere to the rough surface. It should be set about $\frac{1}{4}$ of an inch from the edge all round. Bed this brick so that it rests squarely on its foundation and firmly against the one you have just laid. Quite light pressure only is needed to compress the string and create a seal. Work round the kiln adding one more long and another short brick with similar joints between each, until one course is completed. We have now reached the stage shown in figure 76.

Now prepare for the next layer. Run a short 2 inch piece of asbestos string along each joint as in figure 76A and then the two strips on which to base the next course exactly as before. The joints have to be *bonded* by overlapping as explained in figure 77 so that the one above never coincides with the one below. This makes a strong structure and is the basis of brick-laying. Whenever one brick butts against another there should be a loop of asbestos string to form a rectangular air pocket between the two surfaces. Air, itself, is an excellent insulator and by trapping a little between adjacent blocks, heat is retained and this saves electricity. It would, certainly, be possible to use refractory cement but this requires a good deal of skill and, unless the layer is kept very thin indeed, it tends to crack and becomes a source of heat loss.

When adding the final course, note from figure 77 where the spyhole comes with respect to the base board. It should be on the centre line of the kiln and with its axis $2\frac{1}{2}$ inches from the top. Check that all the brick faces are flush and the walls vertical.

Arrange the four pairs of asbestos side sheets as seen in figure 72 and tie them loosely with a piece of ordinary string to

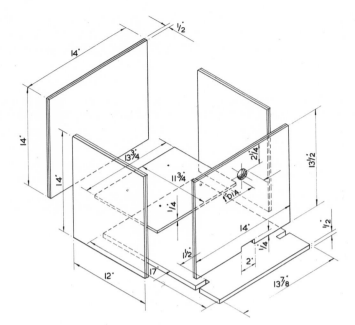

FIG. 72

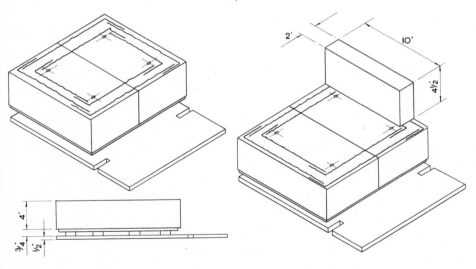

FIG. 73

FIG. 74

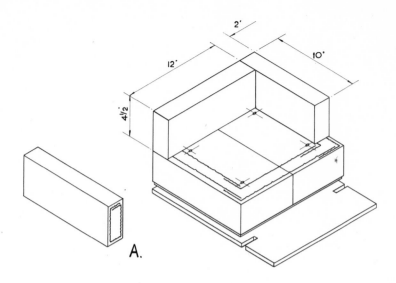

A.

FIG. 75

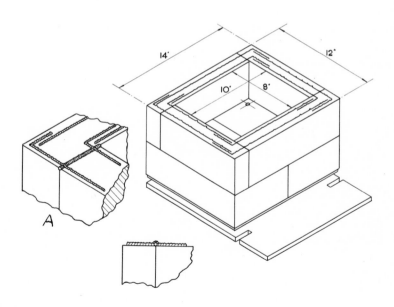

A

FIG. 76

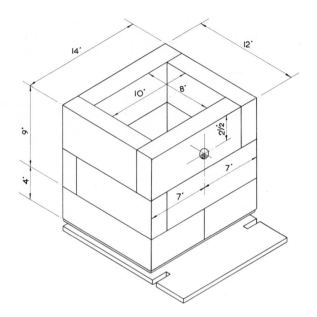

FIG. 77

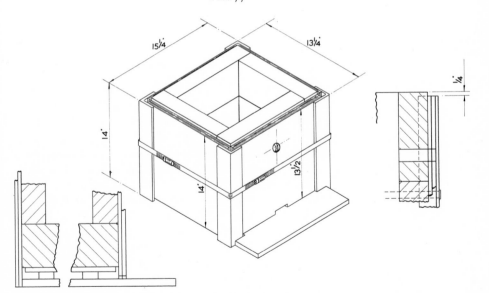

FIG. 78

123

prevent them falling apart, whilst you make sure that they are all going to fit properly. They should not overlap at the corners and when in position should be $\frac{1}{4}$ of an inch below the top layer of bricks. The 12 inch sides pass down to the bottom of the $\frac{1}{2}$ inch base. So does the 14 inch rear pair of panels. The front ones rest on it. Insert the four long angles at the corners so that the whole assembly can be clamped together with the *Jubilee* type clips as shown in figure 78. These latter may reach you each in the form of a circle in which case they have to be unscrewed and joined, the tail of one into the head of the next so as to form a continuous band. Four are required for the kiln body and four for the roof slab (figure 79). Insert a ring of asbestos string between the two

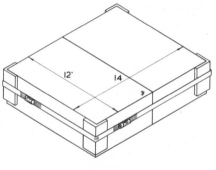

FIG. 79

halves of the roof slab before clamping them together. It will be found easier to screw these up if the worm housing is held with a pair of pliers with one hand and the other wields a screwdriver. Form the band roughly into a rectangle of about the required shape before slipping it over the angles and finally tightening by working progressively round the outside, giving a few turns at a time until everything is quite rigid. It is wise to make certain that there is no sharp edge where the strip bends at a corner. If one is found, either round it off with a file or insert a couple of layers of insulating tape between the two metals to prevent the band being severed when the kiln starts to get hot and expand.

Make a mark on the top slab so that you will be able always to recognise the side which goes over the spyhole. It will then be possible to replace it in that position. Now grind the roof to the main body by repeatedly sliding it backwards and forwards

124

until you are sure that the mating surfaces are in contact. It is only necessary to slide it about ½ an inch each way, applying a little pressure on top as the process proceeds. Later remove the powder so produced by turning the kiln over and brushing it clean. The better the joint you make, the less the heat loss when the kiln is in service.

There are two special element tiles which are used to hold the electric wires. Before these can be wound, however, the spirals have to be prepared. These are made from a material called *kanthal*, which is capable of withstanding extremely high temperatures without melting. The type used for making ordinary electric radiators is not suitable for heating a pottery kiln. When received each element will normally be wound into a tight coil about 26 inches long. This has to be inserted into

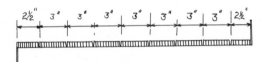

FIG. 80

and distributed evenly throughout nine slots each about 6½ inches long. Begin by dividing the coil into nine segments, one for each slot. The first and the last can be 2½ inches and the intermediate ones 3 inches (figure 80). Do not cut the wire; just separate the coils at the points indicated by slipping in the blade of a blunt knife and twisting slightly to mark the position. Uncoil one turn between the segments so that, when you eventually pull out each to correspond with the length of the slot into which it is to fit, it will appear as in figure 81. It is important that the wire leads directly from one slot to the next and that there are no overhanging loops. This is because, when hot, the *kanthal* softens and will bend under its own weight so ringlets would tend to collapse and touch causing premature failure. When you gently extend the sections, make certain that the spaces are as uniform as possible and that no two turns are in contact. The ends pass through a hole at the extremities of the top and bottom slots and are led down at the back of the tile as shown in figure 82. Note that the two fixing holes for the tiles are placed at the top.

125

Introduce each tile as in figure 81 so that it slides down the short wall of the chamber and the ends of the elements pass through the $\frac{3}{16}$ of an inch holes in the base blocks. They also pass through the $\frac{1}{4}$ inch thick asbestos sheet on which the slabs rest and enter the zone beneath it made by the spacing pads. You will probably have to tip the kiln on to its side to draw the wires taut. Support it on bricks or books so that it rests at an angle to enable you to work comfortably underneath.

Drill two $\frac{1}{8}$ of an inch holes obliquely through the 8 inch wall of the chamber to meet the two in the back of the tile. Cut an $\frac{1}{8}$ of an inch deep groove in the top surface to join them, as is shown in figure 83. This can be done with the blade of a knife or a screwdriver using a ruler as a straight edge. The groove only has to be deep enough to accommodate the short piece of *kanthal* wire which is now used to thread through the holes to keep the tile in position. Twist the ends together as in the drawing and cut off with pliers. This wire is used purely for locating purposes and has no electrical connection with the heating spiral.

The other tile is treated and fixed in exactly the same way.

The tiles are rather delicate and should be treated with extreme care. When both the elements are in place, they should face each other across the kiln and the distance between them should be roughly 8 inches.

Measure the approximate distances from the holes underneath the kiln to where the terminal block will be placed as seen in figure 87. Allow plenty of surplus and cut off four lengths of asbestos covered wire. Scrape off the insulating jacket at one end of each piece along $\frac{1}{2}$ an inch. Loosen the screws in the porcelain connectors (two in each) and slide a connector on to each of the four wires protruding from the underside of the bottom slab. Into the other end of the connector insert the exposed part of the covered wire. The two, thus, overlap inside and when the screws are tightened up there should be a good electrical contact between the ends. Be sure that there is enough of the *kanthal* projecting to allow you to turn the porcelain pieces on their sides so that, when the kiln rests on its spacers, they fit comfortably underneath. Cut off the surplus element close to where it emerges from the connector (figure 84). Finally, lead the four asbestos cables out by way of the notch cut in the outer wall.

The steel terminal box can now be screwed down on to the

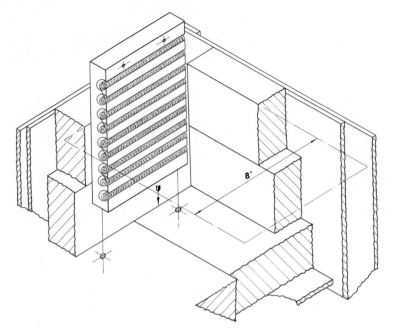

FIG. 81

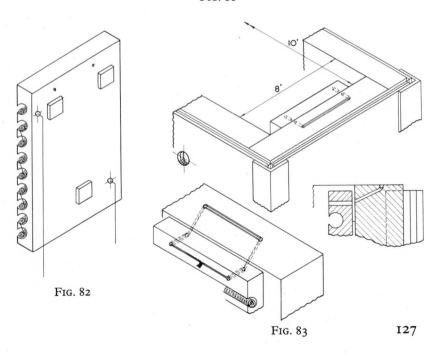

FIG. 82

FIG. 83

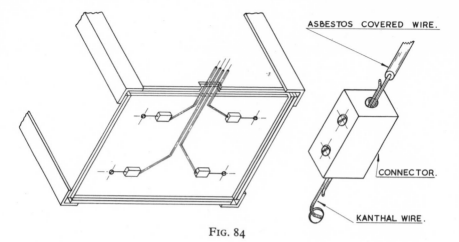

FIG. 84

$\frac{1}{2}$ inch base board as shown in figure 85, having first removed the two knock-out discs (a smart blow with the corner of a hammer head or a heavy screwdriver will easily detach these). There are now two holes in opposite sides through which you can pass the incoming and outgoing cables. Since the edges would be sharp and liable to chafe against the vulnerable insulation, they have to be protected by bushes which have rounded corners. Fit these at this stage and have the nuts inside. The rubber sleeve will grip the incoming three-core flex if both are pulled firmly together through the bush. Bare the three ends of the wires and secure them in the triple block which can then be fixed with a 1 inch No. 6 wood screw which passes through a hole in the terminal box and into the $\frac{1}{2}$-inch board. Check carefully which is the earth (which will be green or green with yellow bands) and lead a bare wire from the earth socket to any spare tapped hole inside the box. Usually there is room for a 4BA setscrew somewhere; if there is not, trap it under a washer at the $\frac{1}{2}$-inch wood screw which holds the box to the board. If all else fails, you can later use one of the ones which are used to secure the cover. Whatever happens, be certain to scrape away all paint, dirt or rust from the point where the earth is to be attached so as to obtain a satisfactory electrical contact. Run another bare lead from the earth terminal out through the bush nearer the kiln and fasten this firmly to the *Jubilee* clip on that side of the kiln. There is a special copper perforated clamping strip which

128

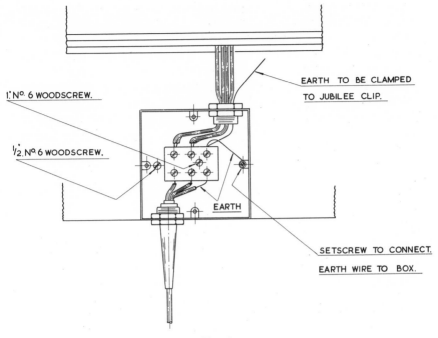

I.́ N.º 6 WOODSCREW.

¹/₂.́ N.º 6 WOODSCREW.

EARTH TO BE CLAMPED
TO JUBILEE CLIP.

EARTH

SETSCREW TO CONNECT.
EARTH WIRE TO BOX.

FIG. 85

can be wrapped round the bulge, housing the little worm
tightening gear as shown in figure 86.

It is now the time to connect up the elements themselves.
Check the lengths of the four asbestos covered wires and remove
about ½ an inch of insulation so that they can be inserted into the
terminals (figure 85). One end of each element goes into the left
hand one and the other ends into the right. They are therefore
said to be wired *in parallel*; the circuit is explained in the Appendix.
Fit the cover on to the terminal block so as to protect all the
exposed electrical parts and your kiln should appear as in
figure 87.

On no account should you connect the equipment to the supply
until it has been thoroughly checked by a professional electrician.
Let him fit the mains plug and confirm that all is well. A thirteen
amp fuse will be sufficient to carry the load.

Before firing your kiln, you will need a stopper for the spyhole.
This can be cut out of a spare piece of insulating brick if you

129

have any surplus. A penknife will do very well and you can finish off with a rough file. Alternatively, a perfectly good stopper may be fashioned out of a wad of *Pyruma* fire cement. Roll it on a hard surface under the palms of the hands or a board, it will set hard quite quickly, especially if gently heated in an oven. Later, whichever material you choose, you can grind the two together by twisting the plug inside the hole so as to secure a reasonably good fit. Remember to leave at least $\frac{3}{4}$ of an inch protruding as the stopper may get very hot later and you will need to grip it with a pair of tongs.

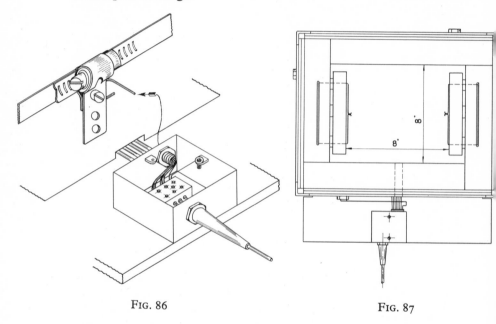

FIG. 86   FIG. 87

Before starting to fire your kiln be sure that you observe the following precautions:

1. Place it well away from anything inflammable or any source of inflammable vapour.
2. Set it on a refractory brick or concrete base, never on a wooden floor.
3. Keep it, at all times, absolutely dry.
4. Never under any circumstances allow children or un-authorised persons to meddle with it.

130

5. Never open the top slab until cool and certainly NEVER when the power is connected to the elements. Always disconnect at the mains.
6. Do not attempt to move the kiln when hot and never do so by lifting only by the ends of the asbestos base board.
7. Beware of the outside surfaces, which, although of insulating material, can become very hot when the kiln is under fire or is cooling down. Any part of the kiln may cause a burn.
8. Always make a habit of using tongs or pliers to remove the spyhole plug.
9. Have the circuit checked by an expert. Never make any alteration to the wiring or try to rectify a fault when the kiln is connected to the power. If in doubt seek advice from an electrician.

The Mini-Kiln is capable of reaching those temperatures which are adequate for so-called *earthenware*. It is not designed for *stoneware*. It will, therefore, fire up to a recommended maximum temperature of about 1170 degs. centigrade. It is true that this limit can be exceeded but by doing so you will, gravely, shorten the life of the electric elements.

Before attempting to use the kiln, inspect all the heating wires to make absolutely certain that they are in their correct slots. Satisfy yourself that no two turns are in contact with each other. Once heated, they become brittle and later on it will be risky to make any corrections.

If you are going to have two layers of ware for your first firing, set three shelf props in position before you introduce any pots. Place the shelf centrally so that there is room for the heat to flow round each of the four sides. You can leave a cone on the floor so that you can inspect it afterwards and later place a second one on the shelf. Having two will help you to gauge the relative temperatures reached by the two halves of the chamber. If you have a range of cones, you can conduct a test by inserting two or three in line, one behind the other, and time their progressive collapses. The *mini-cones* are very convenient for this sort of experiment as, being only $1\frac{1}{4}$ inches tall, they take up much less room. Arrange them so that they collapse away from each other. If necessary, mount them on little mounds of Pyruma cement so that you can see them easily. By adopting this sort of procedure, you will be able to estimate the approximate rate of heat rise in your kiln. Always keep records and then, in the future, you can check the performance and you may be glad to be in a position where you can refer back to what happened at the initial firings. Do not forget that, when there is a heavy charge inside, more heat work has to be done to raise the temperature by the same amount than when the load is light. It is useful therefore to note the number of pots and their weight when keeping such records. As the kiln ages, it may be found that there is a tendency for the firing cycle to alter. If, in time, any cracks start to appear in the refractory, or if the joints seem to have opened a little, it is safe to repair these with a little Pyruma cement. The element tiles can be treated in the same way if they suffer any damage. Be sure, however, to avoid any of the material entering the slots and adhering to the wires.

If you are going to fire pots be sure that, as usual, they are absolutely chalk dry. Keep them well away from the electric spirals. Visualise how the cone or cones will fall so as to be sure that no piece will be touched. Now lift the top slab into place and watch that it sits in the correct relative position to the body of the kiln so that it seals the chamber effectively. The biscuit firing should extend over at least eight hours if the clay is to be properly matured. In any case it is essential to control the rate of temperature rise at first so as to allow the moisture to escape. This can be achieved with a *simmerstat* (suitable controllers of this type are obtainable from the kit suppliers), the wiring connections of which are explained in the Appendix. The device may be fitted to the Mini-Kiln without the additional complication of introducing a relay. If you have no simmerstat, it is still possible to manage quite well by adopting the following cycle:

Switch on for five minutes and off for five minutes twice.
Switch on for ten minutes and off for five minutes twice.
Switch on for fifteen minutes and off for ten minutes once.
Switch on for fifteen minutes and off for five minutes once.
Leave the top spyhole plug out during the above procedure.

If there are still signs of condensation near the hole, then this is a signal that you must continue to be cautious. If not, it is possible to leave the kiln on permanently until the chosen cone has collapsed. To be on the safe side, by making certain that every

132

nook and cranny within the chamber has become hot enough, it is worth firing for a further ten minutes after the bending of the cone. Alternatively, try and maintain the top temperature for a little while by repeated switching off and on in the ratio of 3:2. For example run for fifteen minutes and turn off for ten minutes once or twice. This may seem rather a tedious business, but it is worth the effort. Moreover, it extends the total firing cycle and so ensures better penetration of the heat through the clay. If you are treating pieces with comparatively thick walls, this is more than ever necessary, as it takes time for the temperature to reach right to the interior. Some may argue that a long soak like this may not be particularly good practice when one is working to fine limits of control with special materials and colours, but on the whole it is probably better to chance slight overfiring rather than to risk failure to mature the biscuit. Later, after you have had more experience, you will be able to estimate the liberties you can take. You will also be surprised how accurately the temperature may be recognised just by studying the colour of the pots through one of the spyholes.

Always allow plenty of time for the Mini-Kiln to cool down. Five hours is the very minimum from biscuit temperature, and if you can resist the temptation to remove the top slab under seven, so much the better. When cool, open carefully and inspect the contents for flaws. Any of which have shattered or shed lumps of clay round the thickest parts near the bottoms have probably been too wet or were heated too quickly, or both. Next time make sure that all the ware is drier before placing in the kiln and raise the temperature more slowly. This is done by lengthening the *off* period at the expense of the *on* if you are controlling by hand. With the simmerstat, a lower setting is held longer during the initial stages.

The glost firing is conducted in the normal way. In so confined a space you will have to be more careful than ever that the surfaces do not touch. There is no need to be cautious in raising the temperature. It is, however, wise not to be too reckless, as local stresses may arise which can cause a piece to crack. The bigger the pot the greater the risk of this happening. It is a hazard one encounters in a small kiln where quite wide differences can exist. Some control may, therefore, be found necessary. Start with the plug out until all steam emission has ceased. Once again, do not be in too great a hurry to take off the top. It is well worth waiting a few hours to be certain of not harming any ware.

You can fire on-glaze enamels, gold and silver lustres in the Mini-kiln just as in a full size unit. If you are using these processes, only insert the spyhole plugs after the fumes have been completely eliminated as they tend to affect the electric wires.

In time the elements will have to be renewed. The number of firings you will achieve with each set will depend upon the temperatures reached and the way you have originally arranged them in their grooves. In any case, it is wise always to keep a spare pair available, as usually there is no warning of their life ending, and this avoids the annoyance of waiting for replacements to come through the post. Full instructions for the work of fitting the new ones are supplied with the parts themselves. The main precaution to take is to ensure that the slots are cleared of all traces of the original wire and any other debris. This is a good opportunity to give the interior a thorough spring clean. At the same time, search for cracks and repair them with fire cement.

If you follow the basic rules for firing your kiln and never ill-treat it by cooling it too quickly or allowing the temperature to rise too high, it will give you years of good service. With its aid you should be able to process many hundreds of pots.

APPENDIX I

Technical Data

Approximate squatting temperatures of Seger Pyrometric Cones

No.	Temp.	No.	Temp.
017	730°C	05	1000°C
016	750	04	1020
015	790	03	1040
014	815	02	1060
013	835	01	1080
012	855	1	1100
011	880	2	1120
010	900	3	1140
09	920	4	1160
08	940	5	1180
07	960	6	1200
06	980	7	1230

TYPICAL MOTOR CONNECTIONS.

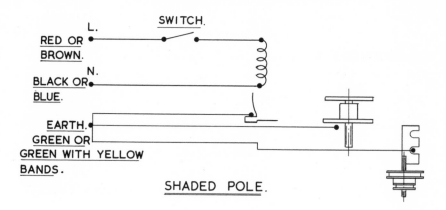

SWITCH.

L.
RED OR
BROWN.

N.
BLACK OR
BLUE.

EARTH.
GREEN OR
GREEN WITH YELLOW
BANDS.

SHADED POLE.

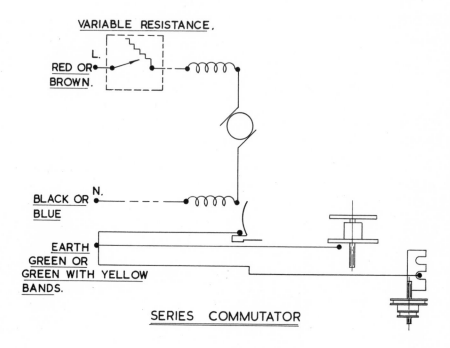

VARIABLE RESISTANCE.

L.
RED OR
BROWN.

N.
BLACK OR
BLUE

EARTH
GREEN OR
GREEN WITH YELLOW
BANDS.

SERIES COMMUTATOR

WAYS OF CONNECTING KILN ELEMENTS.

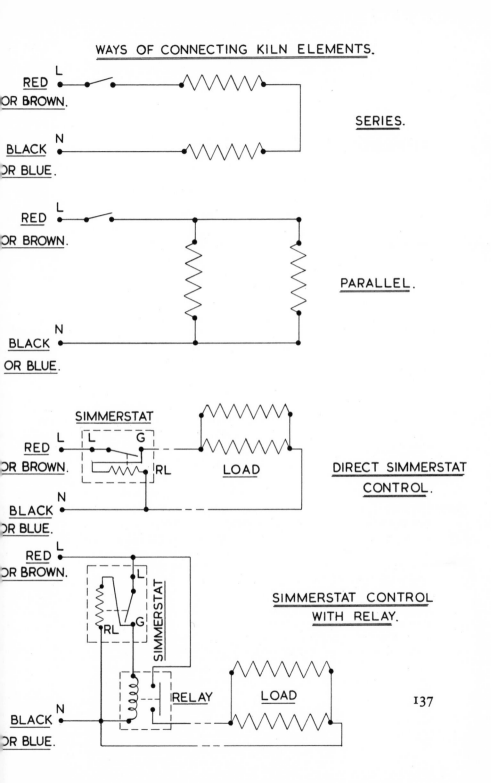

RED
OR BROWN.

L

BLACK
OR BLUE.

N

SERIES.

RED
OR BROWN.

L

BLACK
OR BLUE.

N

PARALLEL.

SIMMERSTAT

RED
OR BROWN.

L

L   G

RL   LOAD

BLACK
OR BLUE.

N

DIRECT SIMMERSTAT
CONTROL.

RED
OR BROWN.

L

L

SIMMERSTAT

RL   G

RELAY   LOAD

BLACK
OR BLUE.

N

SIMMERSTAT CONTROL
WITH RELAY.

APPENDIX II

Some Suppliers of Materials and Parts

A. D. Alpine, 383 Coral Circle, El Segundo, Calif. 90245
Alberta's Ceramic Supply, 5435 N. Peters St., New Orleans, La. 70017
American Art Clay Co., Indianapolis, Ind. 46222
Anderson Ceramics Co., 1950 S. McDuffie St., Anderson, S.C. 29522
Edward Aton, Jr. Ceramic Foundation, 1445 Summit St., Columbus, Ohio 43201
B. & I. Manufacturing Co., Burlington, Wis. 53105
Beckley-Cardy Co., 1900 N. Narragansett Ave., Chicago, Ill. 60637
The Bonnet Co., 825 Lake St., Kent, Ohio 44240
Archie Bray Foundation, Helena, Mont. 59601
Brockton Potters, 17 Nason St., Brockton, Mass. 02401
Gilmour Campbell, 14258 Maiden St., Detroit, Mich. 48213
Capital Ceramics, 2174 S. Main St., Salt Lake City, Utah 84115
Castle Clay Products, 1055 S. Fox St., Denver, Colo. 80223
Ceramic Color and Chemical Manufacturing Co., New Brighton, Pa. 15066
Ceramichrome, Box 2086, Gardena, Calif. 90247
Cole Ceramic Laboratories, Gay St., Sharon, Conn. 06069
Craftool Co., 1 Industrial Rd., Woodridge, N.J. 07095
Crusader Kilns, 1064 Butterworth St., S.W., Grand Rapids, Mich. 49504
Duncan Ceramic Products, 5673 Shields Ave., Fresno, Calif. 93727
Dunham Ceramics, 2870 Milburn Ave., Baldwin, N.Y. 11510
Ettl Studios, Ettl Art Center, Glenville, Conn. 06830
Evenheat Kilns, 6949 Townline Rd., Caseville, Mich. 48725
Gare Ceramic Supply Co., Box 830, Haverhill, Mass. 01830
Holland Mold, 1040 Pennsylvania Ave., Trenton, N.J. 08638
House of Ceramics, 11011 N. Hollywood St., Memphis, Tenn. 38108
Hydor Therme Corp., 7155 Airport Highway, Pennsauken, N.J. 08109
Kanthal Corp., Wooster St., Bethel, Conn. 06801
Kiln Guard, Box 1055, Jacksonville Beach, Fla. 32050
H. B. Klopfenstein, Route 2, Crestline, Ohio 44827
Luckey Laboratories, Luckey, Ohio 43443
Mayco Colors, 20800 Dearborn St., Chatsworth, Calif. 91311
Midwest Ceramic Center, 722 Southwest Blvd., Kansas City, Mo. 64106

Minnesota Clay Co., 2410 E. 38th St., Minneapolis, Minn. 55406
Mixing Equipment Co., 210 Mt. Read Blvd., Rochester, N.Y. 14611
Newton Potters Supply Co., 96 Rumford Ave., West Newton, Mass. 02165
Ohio Ceramic Supply, Box 630, Kent, Ohio 44240
Paoli Clay Co., Route 1, Bellville, Wis. 53508
Peoria Arts and Crafts, 1207 W. Main St., Peoria, Ill. 61606
The Pyrometer Instrument Co., Northvale, N.J. 07647
Rovin Ceramics, 7456 Fenton St., Dearborn Heights, Mich. 48127
Sculpture House, 38 E. 30th St., New York, N.Y. 10016
Skutt and Sons, 2618 S.E. Steele St., Portland, Ore. 97202
Standard Ceramic Supply Co., Box 4435, Pittsburgh, Pa. 15205
Tepping Studio Supply Co., 3517 Riverside Drive, Dayton, Ohio 45405
Triarco Arts and Crafts, Box 106, Northfield, Ill. 60093
Trinity Ceramic Supply Co., 9018 Diplomacy Row, Dallas, Tex. 75235
Unique Kilns of Trenton, 530 Spruce St., Trenton, N.J. 08638
S. Paul Ward, 601 Mission St., Box 336, South Pasadena, Calif. 91030
Westwood Ceramic Supply Co., 14400 Lomitas Ave., City of Industry,
    Calif. 91744
Jack D. Wolfe Co., 724 Meeker Ave., Brooklyn, N.Y. 11222
Zanesville Stoneware Co., 309 Pershing Rd., Zanesville, Ohio 43701
Zirco, 590 S. San Vicente Blvd., Los Angeles, Calif. 90048

GLOSSARY

Bat	A flat piece of wood, tile or plaster which may be in the form of a disc on which clay is thrown on the wheel or left to dry.
Biscuit	Clay which has been once fired in the kiln, but not glazed.
Body	The clay with its additives used in pottery.
Chalk Dry	Clay which has been allowed to stand until it feels perfectly dry.
Coiling	The practice of making pots or other ceramic pieces from strips of clay which are pressed together into a single article.
Collaring	Using the wet hands to make a spinning shape on the wheel smaller in diameter.
Cone	Seger cones are made from special clays and fluxes. They are used to indicate 'heat work' and hence temperature. They bend after a given interval in a kiln.
Course	A layer of bricks.
Element	A coil of special wire through which electricity can be passed to generate heat.
Firing	The art of treating clay and other materials by heat to produce special effects and chemical changes.
Footring	The turned base of a pot.
Glaze	Usually a mixture of a flux and a silicate, possibly with other substances, which will fuse to form a glasslike coating on a pot.
Glost	Firing: the fusing of the glaze when it coats the biscuit in the kiln. Generally the second firing of pottery.
Grog	Finely ground biscuit which is mixed with clay body to make it firmer. Grog has the same firing properties as the body with which it is mixed.
Kanthal	A special electric element wire which will survive in extremely high temperatures, used in good quality kilns.

Leather hard	The state in which clay is rigid without being brittle. An intermediate condition, during drying, when pieces can be handled safely.
Lustres	Also known as *on-glaze enamels*, they are chemicals used for decorating glazed pots. Brilliant effects can be achieved with lustres. To fix them the pot must be refired.
Prop	A ceramic support, usually circular, for a shelf in a kiln.
Relay	An electrical device to enable a circuit carrying a relatively heavy current to be controlled by a circuit carrying a light one.
Sgraffito	The scratching away of a slipped or coloured surface to reveal the body or a different pigment underneath.
Simmerstat	An electrical timing device which can be set to fix the rate of heat release. It does this by rhythmically making and breaking a circuit, the ratio of *on* to *off* being determined by positioning a pointer on a scale.
Slip	A creamy liquid consisting of clay and water sometimes mixed with a pigment.
Slurry	A soft, semi-liquid, mixture of clay and water.
Stilt	A three-cornered ceramic support with pointed feet to prevent glazed pots fusing to kiln shelves.
Throwing	The art of forming pottery shapes on the wheel with the hands.
Turning	The process whereby certain parts of a pot are finished with a cutting tool whilst being spun on the wheel.
Wedging	The continual cutting and mixing of clay to free it from air bubbles and to make it uniform in texture.

INDEX

142